Beyond the ''SP'' Label

Beyond the "SP" Label

Improving the Spelling of Learning Disabled and Basic Writers

Patricia J. McAlexander
The University of Georgia

Ann B. Dobie
The University of Southwestern Louisiana

Noel Gregg
The University of Georgia

National Council of Teachers of English
1111 Kenyon Road, Urbana, Illinois 61801

Staff Editors: David A. Hamburg and Rona S. Smith

Cover Illustration: Carlton Bruett

TRIP Cover Design: Michael J. Getz

Interior Design: Doug Burnett

NCTE Stock Number 02891-3050

Library of Congress Cataloging-in-Publication Data

McAlexander, Patricia J.
    Beyond the "SP" label : improving the spelling of learning
disabled and basic writers / Patricia J. McAlexander, Ann B. Dobie,
Noel Gregg.
        p.   cm.
    Includes bibliographical references (p.).
    ISBN 0-8141-0289-1
    1. English language—Orthography and spelling—Study and
teaching—United States. 2. English language—United States—
Remedial teaching. I. Dobie, Ann B. II. Gregg, Noel. III. Title.
LB1574.M34   1992
428.1—dc20   92-11633
                                                           CIP

Contents

Acknowledgments

We are grateful to a number of people for help with this book. In particular, we thank manuscript consultants Dorothy J. Altman (English, Bergen Community College, Paramus, New Jersey) and Anne Bourgeois (English, Lafayette High School, Lafayette, Louisiana). We also thank those who provided materials, illustrations, information, or other assistance on particular segments of the manuscript: Rosemary F. Jackson (Division for Education of Exceptional Children, The University of Georgia); Irene F. Jewell (Latin, retired from Johnstown High School, Johnstown, New York); L. Milton Leathers III (Athens, Georgia); Connie McDonald (English, Acadiana High School, Lafayette, Louisiana); Gloria Shen (Department of Comparative Literature, The University of Georgia); Keri Turner (technical writing graduate student, The University of Southwestern Louisiana); and Elaine Bond, Christopher G. Hayes, Earl Ginter, Jan Kemp, Jane Marston, and Alexis Winger (Division of Developmental Studies, The University of Georgia).

In addition, we appreciate those who granted us permission to reproduce their unpublished or previously published material: K. F. Anderson, Developmental Studies, Southern College of Technology, Marietta, Georgia, "Individual Spelling Survey" (earlier version published in "Using a Spelling Survey to Develop Basic Writers' Linguistic Awareness," *The Journal of Basic Writing* 6 [1987]: 77); the Gainesville College English faculty, Gainesville, Georgia, "DSE 031 Spelling List"; Janet M. Goldstein, upper school English, Friends Select School, Philadelphia, Pennsylvania, "Spelling Errors from Ninth Graders' Journals"; James K. Warren, cartoon originally published in *Phi Delta Kappan*, May 1988, 638. And we extend a special thank-you to the students whose anonymous essay excerpts helped us tie spelling theory to classroom reality.

Finally, we appreciate the efforts of all those at NCTE who worked with this book, particularly Rona Smith, an insightful reader and meticulous editor.

Introduction

Dick had had little interest in writing throughout high school. Placed in a developmental studies composition program his first year in college, he did not exit into regular courses the first quarter. An introductory essay second quarter revealed spelling as his remaining serious problem, resulting in what appeared to be an unacceptable level of writing. In 342 words, he made the following errors: *desisions (decisions), recieved (received), arrises (arises), there (their), whith (with), wair (wear), cloths (clothes), habbits (habits),* and *feeling (feeling)*—an average of one error for every 38 words.

Tracy, another student in the program, also had an unusual number of spelling errors. She often spelled the same word two or three different ways, even on the same page, and had a striking number of homonym errors. Tracy thought that she was a poor reader (she had been held back in second grade for that reason), but she could write well-organized and intelligent essays on articles in the composition textbook. She blamed herself for her spelling problems and repeatedly resolved to work harder. When she was unable to exit after two quarters, she was evaluated for learning disabilities—and found *not* to be learning disabled. Rather, clinicians diagnosed her current spelling problems as stemming from a visual-processing weakness, which had probably also contributed to her being held back in second grade.

Tom had been accepted to the state university on the basis of very high math scores. However, his verbal scores were low, and he knew he had a serious problem with spelling. Indeed, he felt embarrassed every time he had to write a check. Afraid that he would fail his first-year English courses, he delayed taking them as long as he could.

Charles had been diagnosed as learning disabled (LD) in grade school. He was not hearing or visually impaired, but he had trouble processing oral and written language. Unable to identify the individual sounds within words and relate those sounds to spelling, his writing was filled with unrecognizable versions of words. He entered college in a developmental studies program and worked very hard on his subjects, but counselors there suggested that it might be better for him to seek an alternative form of education.

Arthur, a graduate of a large urban high school, made numerous spelling errors that indicated serious inexperience with Standard English. Placed in a developmental English course in college, he did not receive an exiting grade on his exam. The rules at that time stipulated that to exit, a student could not lose more than 60 points for grammatical and mechanical errors; Arthur lost 79 points—56 for misspellings.

And finally, there was Peter, a talented, literary young man whose themes in English 101, filled with misspellings, received such responses from his teacher as "Excellent discussion. Use your dictionary. *D.*" Not wanting to be evaluated by the school's learning disabilities clinic, Peter dropped out of school when he received a *D* in the course.

The names have been changed, but the students are real—and they illustrate an important fact: that spelling, generally considered a grade school subject, is often a major problem for older writers. Indeed, studies suggest that the problem is getting worse. In the first edition of his *Harbrace Handbook* (1941, iii), John C. Hodges published a top-ten list of student errors, based on an analysis of 20,000 college student themes written in the 1930s. In this list, spelling ranked as the number two problem. In an analysis of 3,000 college student papers written in the 1980s, Robert J. Connors and Andrea Lunsford found that spelling errors had gone "from second to first on the list by a factor of three" (1988, 397, 405–406). Likewise, when Gary Sloan compared 1,000 college freshman themes from the 1950s with 1,000 from the 1970s, misspellings had risen about 300 percent (1979, 156–60). Similar, if not greater, increases are occurring in the writing of high school students.

For many of today's secondary and postsecondary "basic" writers (those students whose writing skills are below their grade level), the spelling problem is particularly severe. Not surprisingly, these poor spellers are often self-conscious and insecure about their writing—in school and in life. And although the technology of word processing can help locate and correct spelling errors, the problem is still not easily dismissed. Students do not always have access to a computer or the word-processing skills to use one. Even if they do, using a spell checker can be a time-consuming process, and spell checkers do not catch all spelling errors. Technology, in short, although a great help, has not yet replaced the writer as the initial composer and final editor.

A major factor underlying the large number of spelling problems is, of course, the difficulty of the English spelling system. However, some individuals have more trouble with this system than do others. One reason is *inexperience* with reading and writing Standard English. Inexperienced students, as Mina Shaughnessy writes, "cannot be expected to make visual [print] discriminations of the sort most people learn to make after years of practice" (1977, 174). Moreover, because many English spelling forms do reflect standard pronunciation, variations in pronunciation—whether due to individual idiosyncracies or dialectal differences—make spelling correctly more difficult.

A second reason some students have spelling problems may be their present or past lack of interest in written forms. These uninterested students could be described as *a*literate; they are able to read and write, but avoid doing so whenever possible. When they do read, these students pay (or have in the past, paid) little attention to the appearance of texts. Some of them, during crucial periods of their education, may have been developmentally delayed; that is, certain cognitive abilities had not developed as fully as those of their peers. Such a lag may have long-lasting effects on academic attitude and performance. Other students may have chronic health, psychological, or attentional disorders that keep them from focusing on writing (or have had such disorders in the past). And some may simply have a visual-processing weakness— they can "see" the printed page, but cannot mentally take in its details effectively. A visual weakness is not as severe as a dysfunction, but it nevertheless can make print-oriented activities (such as spelling) difficult. All these problems are no doubt exacerbated by our increasingly oral/ electronic culture, where, for many, trips to the video store have replaced trips to the library.

Finally, poor spelling may be caused by a learning disability—a serious cognitive dysfunction that causes a significant discrepancy between an individual's estimated intellectual ability (as determined by various tests) and actual achievement. Learning disabled students are now making up an increasing percentage of students in basic writing courses. Some of them, like Charles, have been evaluated and officially diagnosed as LD. They usually have had special instruction in the elementary or middle school years and then have been mainstreamed into regular or, more often, basic writing classes in high school or college. However, students with less obvious problems or less vigilant parents and teachers may have never been evaluated for learning disabilities and thus have never been diagnosed. Their writing weaknesses, which become increasingly apparent at higher levels, often result in their being placed in basic writing classes as well.

Whatever the reason or reasons for students' making numerous spelling errors, we find few teachers giving explicit instruction in spelling at the secondary and postsecondary levels. However, we do find a range of reactions to serious spelling problems. At one extreme are teachers who mark errors with red "sp" labels and lower grades substantially, arguing that such errors are not acceptable in other classes or outside the classroom. One teacher, in fact, responded to the question, "Does spelling count?" with, "Does dribbling count in basketball?" (Conners, 1980, 48). At the other extreme are teachers who virtually ignore spelling errors. In their view, emphasis on mechanics such as spelling alienates students and distracts them from more important aspects of writing, such as the development and organization of ideas.

Paradoxically, both these views of misspelling have validity. As the teachers who lower grades maintain, spelling *does* count, and numerous errors will distract even the most sympathetic reader. Even in subjects other than English, poor spelling can affect grades; in life, it can affect public opinion, jobs, and promotions. Thus teachers *should* respond to spelling errors—but, as we argue in this book, constructively more than punitively. When individual students or an entire class have serious problems in spelling, time should be devoted to instruction that is specifically directed to the types of problems the students have. At the same time, however, as teachers who de-emphasize spelling argue, the expression and communication of ideas and student enthusiasm should be major goals of writing classes. Thus we recommend that teachers embed such spelling instruction in a meaning-centered context, spending relatively short periods of class time on spelling and encouraging draft-writing students to focus on catching errors mainly during the final (proofreading/editing) stage of the writing process. Students are usually appreciative—seldom alienated—when a teacher effectively helps them in a recognized area of weakness.

But, some teachers might ask, what of the composition research that indicates that intensive instruction in mechanics has little effect on student writing? (See Hillocks, 1986, 138–39.) Our answer is that, in such studies, the fault may have been in factors external to the subject matter. Other studies, as well as the testimony of many experienced classroom teachers, show that instruction in spelling can be effective, often eliminating a large percentage of student errors. This book is based on the belief that when secondary and postsecondary teachers read student papers to identify the students' patterns of error and select instructional techniques accordingly, students will respond, using what Mina Shaughnessy terms their "adult power of awareness and self-direction" (1977, 186) to strengthen their areas of weakness. In short, teachers should not reject, but move beyond, the "sp" label.

In this book, we have tried to pull together the information and advice from a number of diverse (and often not very accessible) sources—

from lore to research—to help high school and college teachers implement such a form of spelling instruction both in writing centers and in the classroom. The Theory and Research section explores the history and nature of the English spelling system and the evolution of pedagogical attitudes toward spelling instruction. It also describes the cognitive processes involved in spelling and the effects of weakness or dysfunction in some of those processes. Drawing on this information, the Practice section first presents methods of identifying the nature of students' spelling weaknesses; it then describes a number of teaching techniques and technological aids that can be used with individuals or groups to help basic writers improve their spelling.

1 Theory and Research

BACKGROUND: THE SPELLING SYSTEM

The English spelling system is a complex one; linguist Mario Pei has called it, indeed, "the world's most awesome mess" (1952, 280). This complaint has been echoed time and time again, no doubt often by our students—and with justification. There are, however, some aspects of our spelling system for which they can be thankful. One is the fact that it employs the versatile and relatively simple alphabetic system of writing, rather than the more difficult logographic or syllabary systems.

Alphabetic Systems versus Other Writing Systems

Logographic versus Alphabetic Systems

In the alphabetic system, a grapheme (written sign—i.e., a letter) usually represents one particular phoneme or sound (for example, b = the "buh" sound, as most of us learned in first grade). In contrast, in logographic or pictographic writing, a single grapheme or mark represents an *entire* word or concept. (The term unites *logo*, Greek for *word*, and *graphikos*, Greek for *writing*.) Most words are formed by combining one or more of these graphemes. Chinese writing and a Japanese orthography called *kanji* (borrowed from the Chinese system) are examples of logographic systems. In Chinese and kanji, the symbol ⛰ at one time meant *mountain*, 〰 *river*, ☽ *moon*, and ☉ *sun*. Here, the "picture" quality of the character is clear. Today, however, the symbols have been simplified so that they are more abstract: *mountain* is 山 , *river* 水 , *moon* 月 , and *sun* 日 .

Basic graphemes like these are put together to build other meanings: for example, the three marks— ⌒ (*mound of earth*),

王 *(depth)*, and ＼／ *(nuggets of gold or metal)*—are combined in the character 金 , which represents *gold*. The characters are often metaphorical in nature, also, as illustrated by the sign for *profit*. The sign for *the mature rice plant with grain,* 禾 (*grain* is represented by the top stroke), is combined with the sign for *knife,* リ , to form 禾リ , the sign for *harvest* or *profit*. (Leathers, 1990).

Such logographic writing has some advantages over the alphabetic. First, since logography is not based on the *sound* of the spoken word, speakers of totally different dialects, using different pronunciations or even different words, can usually read each other's logographic writing. Moreover, individuals with an auditory impairment—those unable to hear accurately or to process the meaning of sound—would have less difficulty using such a system than they would using the phonetically oriented alphabetic systems. Finally, logography may be easier for those whose spatial sense is more developed than their lineal sense; for such people, "pictures" are easier to interpret than the sequential sounds.

Gloria Shen of the University of Georgia (1990) relates an incident to illustrate this difference. In Japan, where the logographic kanji (used for words of Chinese origin) is intermixed with phonetic writing systems, a man sustained an injury to the left hemisphere of his brain, the side which deals more with the lineal and rational. The right hemisphere, the more spatially oriented and "artistic," was not injured. Thereafter, he was able to read only the kanji characters, not the phonetic ones. (See figure 1 for an illustration of Japanese writing.)

In most cases, however, using a logographic system is much more difficult than using an alphabetic system. Logography requires far more memorization and visualization. For example, English writers need learn only twenty-six letters; students of Chinese writing must memorize a far greater number of pictorial components of characters and learn to combine those components in hundreds of ways. According to Shen, it takes a Chinese student "eight to ten years of study just to function as a literate person in Chinese society" (1990). It also takes finer motor skills to produce these complex logographic characters than to produce the usual circle, curve, line, and dot combinations of alphabet letters.

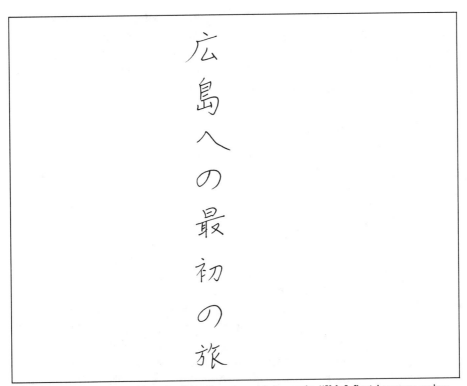

Figure 1. Japanese writing. In this phrase, which reads "[My] first journey going to Hiroshima," the first, second, fifth, sixth, and eighth symbols (from top to bottom) are in the logographic kanji; the third, fourth, and seventh symbols are in a phonetic system. Note the greater complexity of the kanji. (Figure and explanation courtesy of Gloria Shen.)

Syllabary versus Alphabetic Systems

Syllabary systems are phonetic, but they are still more difficult for spellers than are alphabetic systems. As the name "syllabary" suggests, the symbols of these systems represent not individual sounds, but the combination of sounds making up larger elements, the *syllables* of words, usually a vowel sound, or consonant-vowel sound. The Japanese use a form of syllabic writing, *katakana,* mainly to write foreign words that have been adopted to spoken Japanese. This system has forty-six characters (or *kanas*), each representing a specific syllable. For example, アメリカ stands for "ah may ri kah" or *America* (Walsh, 1967; in Hodges, 1941, 4).

Syllabary systems are also more difficult to learn and less versatile than alphabetic systems. In syllabary systems, a larger number of signs must be memorized—in katakana, forty-six as opposed to the twenty-six of the English alphabet. In fact, most languages (including English) have such complex syllabic structures that such a system would involve many signs and be extremely difficult to use.

Differences among Alphabets

Although all alphabetic systems use letters to represent individual sounds, specific alphabets are different. Alphabetic systems differ in appearance and in the sounds they represent; some alphabets include sounds that are not represented in other alphabets at all. Alphabetic writing systems also vary according to the way letters are sequenced to form words. The Arabic system, for example, reads horizontally, from right to left; the Japanese can read vertically, from top to bottom, or horizontally, left to right. The English system (which uses the Roman alphabet), of course, reads horizontally from left to right.

The earliest form of alphabetic writing is found in inscriptions discovered around Mount Sinai, dating approximately from the fifteenth century B.C. In forms used by early peoples of the Eastern Mediterranean, alphabets contained only consonants, leaving the reader to supply the vowels. When the Greeks took over such an alphabet, they used the unneeded consonants to represent vowel sounds. This model was followed by the Romans in their alphabetic system—the ancestor of ours. The Romans had three equal but completely separate versions of the alphabet, each fashioned for use with different writing materials. For carving on marble monuments, they used the form which, with few changes, we use today for our "capitals"; for manuscripts of a "serious, dignified, and official nature," a similar but more rounded form was used—the uncial; and for informal, personal notes and correspondence written in wax with a stylus, there was the cursive, also developed from capital letters but written quickly and marked by roundness and an exaggeration of verticals (Benson and Carey, 1940, 101).

The Germanic tribes evolved the Runic alphabet, using it for inscriptions throughout Scandinavia that date back to the third century A.D. For a time, the Anglo-Saxons in Britain used a Runic system of twenty-four letters to inscribe wooden boards, memorial stones, and metal objects. However, it was soon replaced by the Roman system, partly because of the efforts of Christian missionaries. Figure 2 shows samples of letters from Runic, Roman, Greek, and Arabic alphabets.

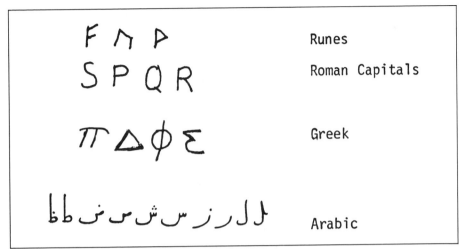

Figure 2. Letters from different alphabets.

The Irregularity of English Spelling

The physical differences among alphabets, however, do not significantly affect the difficulty of spelling. What does affect the difficulty is the closeness of correspondence between the spelling (the series of letters) and the sounds of the words represented. A strict one-to-one correspondence between letters and sounds was named *acrophony* by the Czech linguist Josef Vachek. In some languages, such as Spanish and Italian, the letters of words correspond closely to the sounds of the words; nearly every letter of each word is pronounced. In such systems, writers with good auditory skills can determine the spelling of many words mainly by ear.

Other languages, however, are less acrophonic. In French, for example, a number of letters, especially final consonants, are left unpronounced (*parfait* is *par-fay*). And as we teachers know only too well, English is also one of the languages whose spelling does not strictly correspond to pronunciation. Indeed, of the alphabetic spelling systems, English is one of the most complex. One reason is that the twenty-six letters of the alphabet are used to represent over forty English speech sounds. Thus certain letters represent a number of different sounds (*g* can be pronounced hard, as in *good*, or soft, as in *knowledge*).

But the difficulty of English spelling does not end here: different letters may also represent the *same* sound. For example, the *sh* sound can take any one of several different spellings, as in *mansion, conscious, chaperone, mission, pshaw, nation, suspicion, ocean, fuchsia, shoes,* and *sugar.* George Bernard Shaw pointed out the illogic of English spelling in his famous claim that *fish* should be spelled *ghoti*: the *gh* pronounced as in *rough,* the *o* as in *women,* and the *ti* as in *nation.* English spelling problems are likewise pointed out by the traditional verse:

> Beware of *heard,* a dreadful word
> That looks like *beard* and sounds like *bird,*
> And *dead*: It's said like *bed,* not *bead*—
> For goodness' sake, don't call it *deed!*

In short, an English writer needs to have seen a word, not just heard it, to spell it—for, as Andrew Jackson (one of our less educated presidents) exclaimed, "It is a damn poor mind indeed which can't think of at least two ways to spell any word."

There is still another reason for the lack of one-to-one correspondence between sound and spelling in English: more than many other languages, English is a "melting pot." Although English is a Germanic language, related to modern Dutch and German, it has borrowed heavily from other languages, particularly French and Latin. (Ralph Waldo Emerson once commented, "The English language is the sea which receives tributaries from every region under heaven.") The spelling of some of these borrowed words often diverges from usual English orthographic patterns. A number of such words result from the fact that Renaissance scholars were so enamored of Latin that they altered the spellings of some words to make them reflect their Latin source, even though this meant making the spelling less representative of the pronunciation. Thus we have a number of silent letters—*debt* and *doubt* spelled with a *b, scissors* with a *c,* and *island* with an *s.* English has also incorporated words such as the Greek *pneumonia,* with a silent *p,* or the French *parfait,* with its silent *t,* letters which would normally be pronounced in English. Such inconsistent silent letters in English cause further problems for spellers.

The spelling of borrowed words often violates not only the expected English pronunciation patterns, but sometimes the usual English orthographic patterns as well—as with the Scandinavian word *skiing* (where else in English do you find two *i*'s together?) and the Native American word *canoeing* (very seldom is an *e* kept before an *-ing*). Such exceptions to English spelling patterns and phonics further contribute to the perception that there are no regular patterns to English orthography.

The Standardization of English Spelling

Because of the difficulties in English alphabetic spelling, many weak spellers express the wish that spelling were not standardized, that they could spell a word as they wished to (usually phonetically). However, given individual hearing and pronunciation differences, not to mention dialectal differences, such individual attempts to turn English into a totally acrophonic system would result in a Tower of Babel in written form—a disaster for literacy. Between the thirteenth and the eighteenth centuries, indeed, spelling *was* far less fixed than it is today. Some individuals spelled their names two or three different ways, never thinking anything of it, and spellings varied greatly, with as many as six versions of a word. But during these centuries, a number of influential people realized the importance of a consistent orthographic system and worked to give English one.

Much early credit for standardizing English spelling belongs to William Caxton, a fifteenth-century printer who began consciously representing the words on the pages he printed in a consistent fashion. Although his spelling reflected more his own taste than logic or majority usage, nevertheless, his establishing the principle of consistency was itself a valuable contribution. Other printers followed Caxton's model. By the latter half of the fifteenth century, some 35,000 books had been printed in Europe, and by 1640, over 20,000 printed works had been published in English alone. As the number of printed works increased, spelling forms became increasingly stable.

Although the very printing of the language helped "fix" the spelling, other specific publications attempted to catalog words and find single spellings for words. Two of the earliest efforts were Mulcaster's *Elementarie* of 1582, which attempted to codify usage and spelling, and Robert Cawdrey's *Table Alphabeticall of Hard Usual English Words* (1604), with about 3,000 entries. It was, however, during the eighteenth century that the idea of an absolutely uniform writing system, with a single correct spelling for every word, fully took hold. We find Jonathan Swift arguing in favor of standardized spelling in his *Proposal for Correcting and Ascertaining the English Tongue* (1712): "[The notion that] we ought to spell exactly as we speak . . . [has] contributed not a little to the maiming of the language." Phonetical spelling, declared Swift, destroys etymology and brings about such different spellings that "Writing would entirely confound Orthography." No doubt spurred on by such arguments, Nathaniel Bailey attempted to publish a list of all the words in the English language in his *Universal Etymological Dictionary* (1721). And in 1755 Samuel Johnson published his famous *Dictionary,* a compendium of over 40,000 words, illustrated by 114,000 quotations. For over a century this reference work provided "answers" for English writers anxious to determine proper spelling. The spread of free universal schooling was perhaps the conclusive factor in standardizing spelling. "Correct" spelling became a traditional part of the curriculum, taught, for the most part, by rote memorization and such activities as spelling bees, for which Benjamin Franklin devised rules in 1750. (See Hanna, Hodges, and Hanna, 1971, chapter 6, for a brief history of spelling instruction in America from the eighteenth to the twentieth century.)

The fixed system of spelling clearly did allow individuals to read more easily; they did not have to "translate" the vagaries of individual dialects, at least in most writing, until the appearance of the local-color or dialect tales that were part of the nineteenth-century literary movement termed "realism." In America, these tales were based largely on the frontier oral tradition, as in this passage from George Washington Harris's "Mrs. Yardley's Quilting" (1867):

> Purty soon Sal Yardley started for the smoke-'ouse, so I jis' gin my head a few short shakes, let down one ove my wings a-trailin', an' sirkiled roun her wif a side twis' in my naik, steppin sidewise, an' a-fetchin up my hinmos' foot wif a sorter jerkin slide at every step. Sez I, "Too-coo-took-a-too." She onderstood hit, an' stopt, sorter spreadin her shoulders. (Harris, 1966, 121)

Gradually, however, "oral" literature produced by means of so many phonetic spellings waned in popularity, no doubt because of the difficulty of reading—and writing—it.

Attempts to Reform English Spelling

Although most people accepted the necessity of a standardized spelling system after the eighteenth century, a number of reformers throughout the eighteenth, nineteenth, and twentieth centuries still wished to simplify English spelling by making it more acrophonic. Benjamin Franklin even advocated a new alphabet in 1767, but his suggestion went unheeded. Noah Webster had some success: He insisted that American "honor requires us to have a system of our own, [as opposed to England's] in language as in government," and in his *American Dictionary of the English Language* (1828), he presented simplified "American" spellings of such words as *theater* (instead of *theatre*), *check* (instead of *cheque*), *color* (instead of *colour*), and *wagon* (instead of *waggon*). There were others who attempted reform. In England later in the century, playwright George Bernard Shaw, feeling the need for a way to give his characters valid dialects, fought for a standard phonetic alphabet and left part of his fortune to that end. In 1906 a Simplified Spelling Board was formed in America, and in 1940 the British Simplified Spelling Society worked diligently to secure government approval of a system called "New Spelling."

None of these later attempts to reform English spelling met with any great success, however, and the English spelling system has generally remained unchanged. Because of the desire of scholars to preserve etymologies, the preference of the general public to maintain spelling as it is already known, and, according to some, simple inertia, there have been no mass protests in the cause of simplifying English spelling.

Pedagogical Changes in Views of Error

Although our spelling system has remained virtually the same, educators' views of how much to emphasize grammar, mechanics, and spelling have been changing. In "The Winds of Change" (1982), Maxine Hairston points out that since the 1960s, the traditional paradigm for the teaching of composition has been shifting to a new paradigm, just as in the physical sciences the traditional Ptolemaic model for the solar system shifted to the Copernican.

The Traditional Paradigm

According to the traditional composition paradigm, the written *product* is what is important; thus correctness—freedom from mechanical and grammatical errors—is emphasized. Those who shaped this view were, for the most part, members of English departments of American universities after the 1860s. Harvard gave the view considerable impetus when, in 1874, it instituted an admissions procedure requiring applicants to write a short English composition demonstrating competence in spelling, punctuation, grammar, and expression (Berlin, 1987, 33). Also important in shaping the traditional paradigm were textbook writers of the period, who stressed standards of usage and form. Harvard professor A. S. Hill devoted the entire first part of his influential *The Principles of Rhetoric and Their Application* to surface correctness. In addition, Hill's "English A" course, begun in 1885, emphasized "superficial correctness—spelling, punctuation, usage, syntax—and . . . paragraph structure" in theme writing (Berlin, 1987, 38). This course became a model for similar classes across the country. By the end of the nineteenth century and well into this one, writing classes usually included much formal instruction in grammar, and students were taught to compose tightly structured expository and persuasive themes notable for their mechanical correctness.

The New Paradigm

While a number of teachers and English departments still are influenced by the traditional paradigm, that paradigm has, since the 1960s, been increasingly challenged by a new one. In part, the new views grew out of intellectual developments of the 1960s: linguistics, particularly transformational grammar, began to emphasize process in the development of language, humanistic psychology criticized behaviorist product-response theories, and cognitive psychology investigated how people learn. However, external conditions also played an important role in the change. By the end of the 1960s, educators faced a national decline in conventional verbal skills, open admissions policies in many colleges, increasing numbers of students categorized as learning disabled and as basic writers, and more high school graduates entering college than ever before. Many college freshmen who had "come through schools in which writing had been taught with standard textbooks and standard methods" (Hairston, 1982, 83) seemed to meet none of the traditional standards; some, indeed, appeared, by these standards, to be almost "illiterate" (Shaughnessy, 1977, 3). The new paradigm seemed better equipped to deal with such students.

According to the new paradigm, teachers "cannot teach students to write by looking only at what [the students] had written. [Teachers] must also understand *how* that product came into being and *why* it assumed the form that it did. . . . [They] have to . . . examine the intangible process, rather than . . . evaluate the tangible product" (Hairston, 1982, 84). This approach to teaching composition was promoted by two different "camps" of composition teachers. One was neoclassical in orientation; the other has been called romantic. The former, led by Edward Corbett, James Kinneavy, and Ross Winterowd, among others, reminded teachers that writing is an art of communication first and a demonstration of technical skills second. This group shifted the attention of composition studies to aspects of writing rooted in the writing process, such as invention, the writer's purpose, and the writer-audience relationship. The second camp, led by Peter Elbow, William Coles, Ann Berthoff, and others, emphasized the experience of the writer and the use of writing to define that experience. Language, in this view, becomes a means of self-knowledge and self-creation.

The views of these two camps led to the new paradigm's deemphasis of standard "correctness," for correctness was, after all, not so important in the *process* of writing or in the definition of self. De-emphasizing correctness also seemed appropriate for weaker writers, who, in trying to eliminate errors, often were distracted from developing and organizing their ideas well; moreover, research suggested that formal instruction in grammar and mechanics did little to improve writing. John Butler (1981) illustrates the influence of these views when he describes his decision simply to write on his basic writing students' papers marginal comments like, "All right, I see your point," and "Nice!" without marking errors or giving grades (562–63).

Some advocates of the process-over-product paradigm, however, have resisted such neglect of correctness, however benign. Hairston, for example, writes in another article, "We cannot afford to let students leave our classrooms thinking that surface features of discourse do not matter. They do" (1981, 799). Her survey of eighty-four Texas professionals—administrators, business executives, legislators, and others "in positions to affect other people's lives"—supported her belief; these professionals reacted negatively to a number of the grammatical and mechanical errors she showed them, and "several singled out bad spelling as the most annoying feature they encountered" (798). Now, over a decade later, awareness of the importance of correctness may be returning to "new paradigm" classrooms—but with new approaches to teaching it. In one of the most recent books on the subject, *Grammar and the Teaching of Writing* (1991), Rei Noguchi argues that style is "just as global . . . as organization and content" (13) and that teaching grammar and mechanics *can* help students improve their style. The important thing, argues Noguchi, is not to teach grammar at length and for its own sake, but to make it relevant to the student's writing: teachers should address specifically the problems that crop up most often in student writing and those that society deems most serious.

Perhaps, then, we should regard the shift in composition paradigms as less parallel to the shift from the Ptolemaic to Copernican models for the solar system than to Hegel's system of thesis, antithesis, synthesis. The traditional paradigm, with its concern for the final product, placed too much stress on form, grammar, and mechanics; the new paradigm, the antithesis, so stressed process that teachers sometimes neglected those aspects of writing. We now see, perhaps, a developing synthesis, which combines concern with *both* process and product.

The Paradigms and Spelling

As we suggested in the Introduction, the two opposite views of error we have described are particularly clear in regard to spelling—perhaps the most mechanical of mechanical skills. Traditionally, of course, correct spelling was important. Teachers in high schools and colleges seldom gave explicit instruction in the subject, but they would deal strictly with spelling errors when they occurred. As the new paradigm gained acceptance, correct spelling became, for many English teachers, less important; indeed, errors were sometimes simply ignored.

Ironically, many of the forces that helped bring about the new paradigm also suggest effective methods for teaching spelling. First, cognitive psychology describes the methods or "routes" by which good spellers arrive at a correct spelling. Teachers can employ these insights to give training in specific routes. Second, studies in linguistics have shown that much of our spelling does have logic and order. Patterns of orthographic behavior can be taught to students through spelling lessons and spelling rules. Finally, the new paradigm's pragmatic focus on process and on individual needs can be used, not lost, in teaching spelling. Teachers can find in drafts of student papers the words to teach and the patterns of misspelling to emphasize, thus making spelling lessons for particular students or classes relevant; and they can encourage students who are writing compositions to wait to *focus* on spelling until the proofreading and editing stages of the writing process.

We will discuss such techniques in chapter 2. But first we will show how the changes in the secondary and postsecondary student populations, the classification of an increasing number of students as LD or basic writers, and the insights of cognitive psychology relate to the effective teaching of spelling at the high school and college levels.

CURRENT THEORY AND RESEARCH: THE SPELLER

Every composition classroom, of course, has its misspellers, but these students do not all misspell in the same way. Their work is often dominated by different error patterns, suggesting different problems at the root of their difficulty. For example, Charles, the learning disabled student described in the Introduction, had little sense of the sound of words; he might write *gril* for *girl* or *entisignia* for *anesthesia*. Tracy, on the other hand, spelled words mostly as she heard them, with little sense of whether or not they *looked* right; *possibly* was *possobly* and *especially* was *expecially*. What are teachers to make of the variety of misspellings they find on student papers? And how can they help the students improve?

Current theory and research give direction to teachers trying to assess the spelling needs of their students. Theories of the cognitive processes involved in spelling suggest ways to diagnose the nature of a student's spelling errors, while research on the differences in the spelling errors of learning disabled writers and basic writers helps teachers tentatively identify LD students in their classes.

Common Spelling Routes

According to current cognitive theory, there are a number of ways (or "routes") by which the normally achieving writer arrives at the correct spelling of a word. The two major routes, which usually check and balance each other, are *auditory* and *visual.* Writers use the auditory route when they sound out a desired, or "target," word: *cat+a+log* for *catalog.* Writers use the visual route when they "see" a mental picture of the target word or jot down possibilities and recognize the correct spelling: *catalog* looks right, while *katalog* does not. This sense of the visual apparently arises from "covert memory," an unconscious storing of word images from one's reading which form what has been termed an "internal lexicon." Since neither the auditory nor visual route will be 100 percent accurate even in the best of circumstances, good spellers combine the two in a checks-and-balances system. We might imagine the combined use of these two routes as an old-fashioned balanced chemist's scale.

Other spelling routes supplement these two major ones. These we might think of as weights, which, placed on the lighter side of the scale, help improve and maintain the balance. Some of the most common supplementary routes include the following:

1. **Spelling Rules.** Writers come to recognize, or are taught to recognize, certain spelling patterns in English. They learn, for example, that verbs with a final *e* (*like*) drop the *e* when adding *-ing* (*liking*) and look strange if the *e* is not dropped (*likeing*).

2. **Semantics.** Influenced by their educational and reading background, writers may allow a word's meaning to play a role in its spelling. For example, when using a homonym (the most common term for words that sound alike but are spelled differently and have different meanings), most writers are aware of which spelling they must choose because of its meaning (they know that *too,* not *to,* means *also*). We define this route as also including a knowledge of "semantic cores" or word roots: a writer learns that the spelling of words derived from a common semantic core is often related (*annual, annuities*).

3. **Morphology.** The spelling of many words can be determined by adding suffixes and prefixes to these semantic cores (*dress— dressed, dresser*).

4. **Analogy.** Writers may spell unknown words (*buzz*) by making analogies to the spelling of already known words which sound similar (*fuzz*).

5. **Motor Movements.** Often writers automatically write words, through physical memory, without consciously thinking of the spelling.

See figure 3 for a chart of these routes, and figure 4, to see how a weak speller might use supplemental routes to avoid overreliance on one major route.

Types of Spelling Errors

Unfortunately, as we have seen in the misspellings of Charles, Tracy, and in fact, all other students, every spelling route is subject to error. Indeed, misspellings can be categorized according to which of the two *major* spelling routes (auditory or visual) the writer has overrelied on (the resulting imbalance producing the error) or which relevant *supplementary* route the writer has misapplied or not applied when he or she should have. These categories are not always mutually exclusive, since errors, like correct spellings, can result from the simultaneous use (or misuse) of more than one route. Moreover, two different, separately applied routes might result in the same misspelling. A teacher can, however, usually discern which route played the primary role in producing the spelling error, either by talking with the speller to discover the thought processes involved or by analyzing enough of the speller's errors to recognize patterns of weakness.

It is important, then, for teachers to be familiar with some common categories of spelling errors. (Lists and definitions of some of the following categories are found in Cromer [1980, 412] and Gregg, Hoy, and Sabol [1988, 18].)

The two major categories of spelling errors are related to the two major spelling routes—the auditory and the visual.

Auditory errors, the most common, are so named because they occur when the speller overrelies on the auditory route, neglecting the visual route. The individual's spelling system thus becomes like an unbalanced scale, with "hearing" being far too heavy on its end. As we have seen, this was the case with Tracy, who based her spelling of *possibly* (*possobly*) and *especially* (*expecially*) mainly on the way the words sounded to her. Apparently, to Tracy, *possobly* did not look odd

---

THE TWO MAJOR ROUTES
CHECK AND BALANCE EACH OTHER

VISUAL ROUTE   +   AUDITORY ROUTE
Example: *license*   Example: *license*
(looks right)   (sounds right)

AND ARE OFTEN SUPPLEMENTED BY ONE OR MORE
OF THE FOLLOWING ROUTES:

RULES—Writer applies taught or recognized English spelling patterns relevant to
target word. Example: *receive* ("*i* before *e* except after *c*" rule)

SEMANTICS—Writer uses the meaning of the target word (by recognizing roots and
homonyms) to arrive at spelling.
Examples: using *to* (not *too*) go
recognizing *psyche* in *psychology*

MORPHOLOGY—Writer adds suffixes and prefixes to form target word.
Example: *barbecue + ed = barbecued chicken*

ANALOGY—Writer uses words similar to target word in sound as models.
Example: *all wrong = all right*

MOTOR—Writer uses familiar, hence automatic, movements in writing letters of target
word.
Examples: *feel good*   (e's and *l*'s formed correctly)
                 a factor   (no extra or missing letters)

Figure 3. Common spelling routes.

with the *o* or *expecially* with the *x*. Auditory errors tend to occur when the writer's visual route is weak. Perhaps the writer has a poor visual memory or has not read enough to have the mental pictures of words necessary to balance the auditory route.

Students who spell phonetically tend to write as if they were transcribing a voice in their heads. Since the voice the student is transcribing usually represents the student's own or the voices of those he or she is most used to hearing, auditory errors may be based on an individual's pronunciation idiosyncrasies, as with Tracy's *expecially,* or on geographical variations, as with the student from the Northeast who wrote *displace* for *displays* and the student from the South who wrote *steal* for *still.*

Auditory errors may also include "folk spellings." These occur when the target word is one students have heard but have not seen or cannot visualize; thus they "invent" a spelling based on words already in their lexicon—for example, *could of* for *could've*, *peaked* for *piqued*, *disco tech* for *discotheque, valid victorian* for *valedictorian,* and *Hell, Mary* instead of *Hail Mary.*

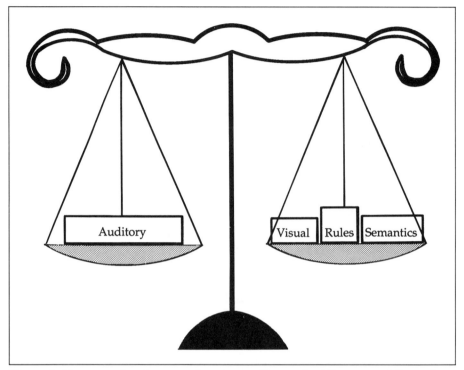

Figure 4. Compensating for a weak major spelling route. When one of the major routes is weak, writers often maintain balance by using the supplementary routes. This drawing illustrates how someone whose visual route is weak uses rules and semantics to keep from making too many auditory errors. (Graphics by Keri Turner.)

Finally, misspellings due to the erroneous splitting or joining of words (*all though* for *although, alot* for *a lot*) are often auditory errors: the writer does not think of how the words look, but of how they sound (*alot* is spoken as if it were one word, an adverb, rather than an article and a noun). Sometimes the writer also misuses sound analogies in making such errors (see subsequent discussion of analogy errors).

Visual errors are so named because they result from overreliance on the visual route, without the appropriate balance of the auditory. (The scale has become unbalanced in the other direction.) In a writer's attempts to reproduce a word's appearance, letters may be added, omitted, or transposed (*answewer* for *answer, may* for *many, hosiptal* for *hospital*). Individuals with auditory weaknesses (such as an inability to match sounds with letters consistently and accurately) will repeatedly make such errors, while students able to balance their inaccurate visual memories of words with the auditory route might spell *girl* instead of *gril* and come closer to *anesthesia* than *entisignia*.

When supplemental routes are misused or not used when they need to be, they can, like misused or missing needed additional weights on the scale, contribute to imbalance. Many spelling errors can be categorized according to the specific supplemental spelling route that was misused or not used when it should have been:

1. **Spelling rule errors** occur when the student is not familiar with or does not recognize certain basic English spelling patterns—like dropping the *e* before adding *-ing* (hence getting *likeing* for *liking*). Spelling rule errors can be the result of either a visual-processing weakness or a gap in the student's education, or, of course, a combination of the two.

2. **Semantic errors** are found when the student, while writing a homonym (*led*) does not consider the word's meaning, but only its sound, and thus selects the wrong "sound-alike" (*lead*). These errors are often a specific form of auditory error, for the writer is generally transcribing the sound of a word, using the first spelling that comes to mind, i.e., the most immediate version of the word in his or her "internal lexicon."

   A semantic error may also, according to our classification, result from the student's not knowing the root of a word. A student's not recognizing the Latin *annus* (*year*) as the root of *annuities* will have trouble determining how to spell the word according to sound; a student who does not know that a root in *psychology* is the Greek *psyche* (mind or soul) will have trouble trying to visualize the order of the initial letters. A variation on this type of problem occurs when a student confuses semantic roots—for example, using the prefix *mini* instead of the root *minu* for the word *minuscule* (thus writing *miniscule*) (Conley, 1974, 245). Semantic errors may indicate an educational or visual weakness, or a combination of the two.

3. **Morphological errors** result when the student omits prefixes and suffixes from root words (*can goods* for *canned goods, girl* for *girls*) or spells the prefix or suffix incorrectly (*dissapointment* for *disappointment, beautifull* for *beautiful*). When the student never "sees" that a final *-ed* or *-s* is missing or added, or that *dissapointment* looks strange, the misspelling is a form of visual error. When the student misspells or omits a prefix or suffix in accordance with his or her way of saying the word, the error is a type of auditory error. Some students often omit the final *-s* on plural nouns, for example, while *-ed* endings on participles are frequently omitted in standard oral speech. Thus *can goods* has become a common pronunciation, and is in fact sometimes used on signs in grocery stores.

4. **Analogy errors** occur when the writer bases the spelling of the target word on a known word that has a similar sound. (*All right* is analogous in sound to *already, high school* to *highway, quiz* to *fizz*—so the writer writes *alright, highschool,* and *quizz.*)

5. **Motor errors** are of a different nature from the others; more physical than perceptual or cognitive, they occur when writers make inappropriate motor movements, so that the *o*'s look like *u*'s and *e*'s like *l*'s, or they write *their* instead of *the* as the fingers automatically continue writing in familiar patterns. Although teachers need to be aware of motor errors, they should realize that such errors are more like typographical errors than real misspellings. Of course, if writers do not "see" the error, the problem becomes visual as well as motor.

For a summary and additional examples, see figures 5 and 6.

Probably the high school and college students who make the greatest number of these spelling errors are those termed "basic writers."

Basic Writers

Characteristics of Basic Writers

Since the late 1960s, a growing number of students at the secondary and postsecondary level have been designated as "basic writers." As Glynda Hull and Mike Rose point out, these writers are also variously called "remedial," "underprepared," "underachieving," "inexperienced," "developmental," or "at-risk" (1989). Sometimes when they are in college, they are called "college preparatory." Students are categorized by one of these labels when they perform below a school-defined level on standardized tests or on writing samples, or sometimes on the basis of teacher recommendations. However they are identified and whatever the label used, these students are not writing as expected for their educational level. Many of these students are placed in variously labeled classes designed to help them come closer to or catch up to their "normally achieving" counterparts.

Of course, different schools use different standards to define the "expected" educational level. One school's basic writer may be another school's average or even advanced writer. The increasing diversity of basic writers can be seen mainly in the changing populations in these programs at postsecondary institutions. Mina Shaughnessy, a pioneer in the field of basic writing, was influenced by K. Patricia Cross's descriptions of "New Students" at the postsecondary level (1971), but she drew mostly from her own experiences with the new open admis-

THE MAJOR TYPES OF ERRORS ARE CAUSED BY
OVERRELIANCE ON ONE OF THE TWO MAJOR ROUTES:

VISUAL ERRORS
Writer overrelies on
   visual route.
Example: *liense*
(no sense of missing sound)

AUDITORY ERRORS
Writer overrelies on
   auditory route.
Example: *lisense*
(no sense of wrong appearance)

OTHER MORE SPECIFIC ERROR TYPES ARE CAUSED BY MISAPPLICATION OR
NONAPPLICATION OF RELEVANT SUPPLEMENTAL ROUTES:

RULE ERRORS—Writer violates a standard English spelling pattern.
   Example: *recieve* (violates *i* before *e* rule)

SEMANTIC ERRORS—Writer does not consider the meaning of a homonym or does
   not recognize a word root.
   Examples: *too* go for *to* go
         physcology for *psychology*
         (no recognition of the *psyche* root)

MORPHOLOGY ERRORS—Writer has incorrect or missing prefixes or suffixes.
   Example: *barbecue chicken* for *barbecued chicken*

ANALOGY ERRORS—Writer uses an inappropriate phonetic model for target word.
   Example: Using *already* as a model for *all right* to get *alright*

MOTOR ERRORS—Writer makes inappropriate physical movements in writing target
   word or its letters.
   Examples: *fell good*   (letters formed incorrectly: *l* for *e*)
         and factor   (extra letters: *and* for *a*)

Figure 5. Common spelling error types.

MISSPELLED WORD	TARGET WORD(S)	PROBABLE ERROR TYPE(S)
intrest	interest	auditory (pronunciation)
whith	with	visual
compareing	comparing	rule
cocach	coach	visual
She staired at me.	stared	semantic
use to	used to	morphological
highschool	high school	auditory/analogy
sociolog	sociology	visual/motor
wich	which	auditory (if writer does not pronounce *h* sound) or visual (if writer does pronounce the *h*)

Figure 6. Classifying spelling errors according to route. Some misspellings can be classified as more than one type of route error. The actual route(s) involved can be determined by ascertaining the thought processes of the speller. Interviews with the writer, or the writer's spelling-error patterns, usually indicate the most accurate classification of ambiguous errors.

sions students in the City University of New York (CUNY) when, in the late 1970s, she described college basic writers. In her bibliographic essay (1976), Shaughnessy suggests the backgrounds of these students: "We can infer that they have never written much in school or out, [and] that they have come from families and neighborhoods where people speak other languages or variant . . . forms of English" (139). As for their writing, their "difficulties with the written language [seem] of a different order from . . . other groups. . . . The inexperienced teacher is almost certain to see nothing but a chaos of error when he first encounters their papers" (1977, 2, 5).

But throughout the 1980s, as Andrea Lunsford and Patricia A. Sullivan point out in "Who Are Basic Writers?" (1990), "the impact of open admissions in particular and broader access to higher education in general" greatly increased the numbers of postsecondary basic writing students. The meaning of the term, in short, broadened to include students "from every avenue of American public education; students in basic writing classes, depending on the college or university, were almost as likely to have graduated from an elite private school as from a large urban ghetto school" (18).

Thus the abilities of today's college basic writers vary greatly. In a number of schools, for instance, basic writing classes include the students Shaughnessy described as one "group" above her basic writers, students who had, in Shaughnessy's words, "survived their secondary schooling but not thrived on it, whose reading [is] seldom voluntary and whose writing [is] . . . by no means error-free but limited more seriously by its utter predictability—its bare vocabulary, safe syntax, and platitudinous tone. . . ." (1977, 2). And when Lynn Quitman Troyka (1987) examined a national sample of basic writers' essays (109 essays from twelve colleges in various areas of the United States and Canadian provinces), she was struck by the "dramatic" differences among them, both in weaknesses and in strengths (11).

At the high school level, the students referred to as basic writers are usually found in below-average or "practical" classes (the label varies). However, high school students in average or even advanced English classes may be placed in basic writing classes in college.

Thus the term "basic writer" has become a very broad one. The expansion of the term is reflected in a statement in *The Journal of Basic Writing*'s call for articles (written in 1984 by then editor-designate Troyka): "The term 'basic writer' is used with wide diversity today, sometimes referring to a student from a highly oral tradition with little experience in writing academic discourse, and sometimes referring to a student whose academic writing is fluent but otherwise deficient" (quoted in Troyka, 1987, 4).

It is difficult today, then, to generalize about the backgrounds and abilities of students designated as basic writers. However, we believe that it is possible to suggest some reasons for these students' being deficient, if in varying degrees, in expected writing skills at both the high school and college levels. To begin, there is the inexperience described by Shaughnessy. In addition, some of these students may have weaknesses in cognitive areas (such as auditory or visual processing) which affect their writing. Some may lack motivation and interest in school or be chronically fatigued. Some may have been developmentally delayed during important periods in their grade school education and so never fully mastered the fundamentals taught during that period. Some may have chronic health, attentional, or psychological problems, or have had such problems during a significant period of their education. Some may even have all of the above. Figure 7 lists these reasons. In many cases, it is very difficult to determine which of these factors resulted in a particular student's writing difficulties.

The Spelling of Basic Writers

Many basic writers, as we have seen, have serious problems with spelling. The following student passage from Shaughnessy's *Errors and Expectations* exemplifies some types of misspellings basic writers may make:

> . . . I *fell* that *seeig* and hearing has the same quality to both infants and parents. . . . [T]hey both appreciate, just because there aren't that many *panters* or musicians around *dosen't* mean infants are more sensitive to beautiful than *there* parents. (1977, 8— misspellings emphasized by us)

This writer has five misspellings in thirty-nine words: four seem to be motor and/or visual errors (*fell, seeig, dosen't,* and *panter*), and one is a typical homonym error (*there*). The writer also seems to have omitted a word: unless the error is one of syntax, a noun is needed after "beautiful"—an error indicating a visual-processing weakness.

Another student sentence, this one quoted in a Hull and Rose study (1989) gives us further examples of basic writers' spelling errors. This student writes:

> This something telling about a nurse who *won't* to help a *patience.* (146—misspellings emphasized by us)

Here again, we see an omitted word; there are also two homonym/

1. A Cognitive Weakness (in spelling, particularly an auditory or visual-processing weakness)
2. Learning Disabilities (a cognitive area may be dysfunctional)
3. Inexperience with Standard Written English
4. Health, Attentional, or Psychological Problems (past or present)
5. Lack of Motivation
6. Developmental Delay (usually in the past)
7. Fatigue

Figure 7. Possible reasons for the writing deficiencies of basic writers.

near-homonym errors, which may be morphological errors as well. (*Won't,* for *want,* suggests the omission of the third person *s* ending; *patience* adds an incorrect *s* sound to the end of *patient.*)

Finally, we have this passage, from one of our students, with the errors italicized:

> In a dorm however one has a *roomate* to share a room *bairly* big enough for one person. If one wants to study, they must go to the study lounge which is *inconvenyent.* . . .

The three misspellings in these thirty words accurately reflect the sound of the target words, but apparently none of these spellings *looked* odd to the writer.

Many such misspellings can be explained, we think, in terms of the reasons we've given for basic writers' general difficulties with writing. Often, their spelling errors indicate an overreliance on oral language. Some of the students show inexperience with both the sound and sight of Standard English; others show experience with *hearing* it but little with seeing it. Omitted words and the production of idiosyncratic spellings also may indicate visual-processing weaknesses that keep students from "taking in" printed words. Sometimes a developmental delay in reading and writing in a student's earlier years is the source of spelling problems. Finally, spelling errors may also reflect haste and carelessness arising from a lack of motivation or an attentional, physical, or psychological problem.

Not all the work of basic writers will have as many spelling errors as do the writing samples given here. In fact, basic writers are often able to avoid numerous spelling errors because they use simple words they know how to spell or spend an inordinate amount of time checking their spelling. Helping these basic writers build their spelling skills will not only eliminate many of the mistakes they do make, but also allow them to give more of their energy and attention to broader matters of writing and to feel less restrained in their word choice.

Learning Disabled Writers

The writers who have the most trouble with spelling are often those who, like Charles, are learning disabled. A student is so diagnosed when a psychoeducational evaluation indicates a severe discrepancy between intellectual potential and achievement, a discrepancy that cannot be explained primarily by environmental or emotional factors or by external physical disabilities. In these cases, the specific cognitive difficulties are assumed to have a neurological basis.

Although one could say that the term "learning disabled" is a label just like the term "basic writer" (or its variants), there are important differences. Whereas "basic writer" is an institutional and departmental label usually defined and temporarily applied (for placement purposes) by the English faculty of the institution the student attends, "LD" is a label that indicates a probably permanent neurological condition, and that has political and legal ramifications. (Federal law requires public schools to serve students identified as LD, and schools receive some reimbursement for their expenses.) Moreover, for legal purposes, this label can be assigned only by a group of certified experts in the field (usually clinical psychologists, educators, LD specialists, and speech and language specialists). Although the input of the student's teachers is considered, the assessment team is usually external to secondary and postsecondary English faculty.

Because students are labeled LD by specialists, because the concept of learning disability assumes a neurological dysfunction, and because LD students are categorized as disabled, along with the physically impaired, some people think that learning disabilities should constitute an objectively verifiable physical condition that one tests in the same way that medical doctors test for diabetes or X-ray for broken bones. As a matter of fact, current technology, such as positron-emission tomography (a form of CAT scan), magnetic resonance imaging (MRI), and ultrasonography, along with autopsies, has begun to reveal asymmetries and deviations in the brains and brain functioning of individuals diagnosed with some types of severe learning disabilities. As our technology becomes more advanced, such deviations may be recorded in individuals with more subtle and complex learning disabilities as well.

So far, however, these techniques have been used not for diagnosis, but mainly to verify and explore the differences in the brains of individuals already diagnosed as learning disabled. For actual diagnosis, LD assessment uses psychoeducational techniques to evaluate students who are referred usually because they exhibit performance problems in school. There are, of course, in this rapidly developing field, a number of issues still to be resolved about LD evaluation and a number of models of assessment. In general, however, LD assessment teams conduct interviews with the student and others, observe his or her behavior patterns, and administer various psychological, physiological, and cognitive tests. Then, on the basis of all data (both qualitative and quantitative), they arrive at a conclusion about the person's condition. (See Smith, 1991, 306–43, for a detailed description of LD assessment in schools, and McAlexander and Gregg, 1989, for a description of the evaluation of two students at a state university's learning disabilities center.)

Occasionally, one member of an evaluation team may determine that a student is not learning disabled, another that he or she is; or members may not be able to agree on precisely what specific cognitive dysfunction the disability stems from. However, just as in the medical and psychological (and, for that matter, educational) professions, if diagnostic disagreements occur, they are usually in particularly complex or borderline cases. In the majority of cases, LD assessment team members agree that a student is learning disabled and then reach a consensus upon the nature of his or her dysfunction(s). Most English teachers have taught students who have been thus identified as LD; they have seen that although these students are often bright, their learning problems are unusual, their thought processes different. In short, although the LD diagnosis works as an educational label, it is more; and although the diagnosis is seldom physically verifiable, most professionals involved with LD students assume that it does reflect a neurological reality.

We, too, accept that assumption. But more important, we believe that, for all their differences, students diagnosed as learning disabled have characteristics and needs that often overlap with those of basic and even regularly placed writers. Indeed, increasing numbers of learning disabled students are found in basic writing classes. One reason is that, by the 1980s, increasing numbers were diagnosed and given special instruction in elementary school. Improving their skills enough to be mainstreamed, they have been entering high school and college classes, but often those for basic writers. Along with them in these classes are students who have never been evaluated for possible learning disabilities, but whose LD symptoms are beginning to appear in their writing as writing demands increase. Thus we include LD students in this book. In the following sections, we describe the LD concept, common characteristics of LD writing, and some specific subtypes of disability that involve problems with spelling.

Characteristics of Learning Disabled Writers

Most of today's teachers of basic writing have accepted the concept of learning disabilities and the possibility that a number of their students, whatever their background, may have some kind of diagnosed or undiagnosed cognitive dysfunction. Teachers still may not, however, be aware of some specific traits and types of these students as writers. The learning disability they hear about most often is dyslexia. Derived from the Latin *dys* (*bad* or *difficult*) and the Greek *lexis* (*word*), the term refers to problems in *reception* of written language (i.e., reading). Dyslexia is also popularly used to refer to writing disabilities because most dyslexics have corresponding problems with the *expression* of written language. However, not all individuals with writing disabilities are dyslexic. Some individuals can read and understand written language but not produce it, can follow and appreciate organization patterns but not write clearly organized essays, can read words but not be able to spell them. Cases of individuals with brain injuries who can read but not write show that reading and writing abilities are separate. Therefore, the condition involving difficulty with writing skills is more accurately termed *dysgraphia* (from *dys*—*bad* or *difficult*—and the Greek *graphikos*—*writing*).

Although every person diagnosed as learning disabled is unique, dysgraphic writers often display certain specific characteristics. Because these individuals frequently have motor or hand-eye coordination problems, their handwriting may be unusual in some way—perhaps all in capital letters, or in rounded grade school printing, or in a sloppy cursive with letters merging into each other or otherwise malformed (*n*'s become *m*'s, *o*'s become *u*'s, *e*'s become *l*'s). In addition, the organization of their papers may have serious lapses; their tone or word choice may be inappropriate, their syntax confusing, and their mechanical errors not only more frequent, but also not necessarily attributable simply to inexperience with Standard Written English. One of the most recurring indicators of dysgraphia, however, is misspelling.

The Spelling of Dysgraphic Writers

A severe spelling weakness seems to be one of the most persistent signs of dysgraphia. Indeed, spelling errors can be like a window to the mind, for they indicate not only the existence of a learning disability, but also its nature. Teachers need to be aware of three common characteristics of the spelling of LD writers:

1. **High Frequency of Errors.** The first characteristic of dysgraphic spelling is an unusually high number of spelling errors. Studies show that, in general, writers diagnosed as dysgraphic make more spelling errors than other basic writers—both in recall tests and in spontaneous writing. Gregg, Hoy, and Sabol (1988), in a study of thirty-five normally achieving writers, thirty-five basic writers, and thirty-five LD writers at a large Southeastern university, discovered that, on the WRAT-R (a spelling recall test) LD writers had the lowest scores, and in a spontaneous writing sample, they made "significantly more spelling errors" than writers in the other two groups (21).

2. **Unusual Errors.** A second characteristic of dysgraphic spelling is that the errors are particularly unusual; indeed, the term "bizarre" is often applied. Amy Richardson (1985), contrasting "errors of inexperience" with "errors of writing disability," states that, although some errors overlap, writing disabled students "will also misspell words in other . . . unpredictable ways [that] . . . cannot be associated with causes such as transference of pronunciation or dialect variants, ignorance of spelling rules, or some factor that causes a *widespread* tendency to misspell. The characteristics of the misspellings of writing dysfunction are seemingly *random* distortions, letter reversals, and the dropping of end letters" (71, emphasis ours).

   Often the misspellings are fairly rare: *ock* for *oak, wieddle* for *widely, entisignia* for *anesthesia.* Christopher Lee, a student diagnosed as LD, reports that his spelling was so bad that when his friends tried to "decipher my notes to quiz me for a test, they [had] no idea what language I [was] writing in" (Lee and Jackson, 1992, 26).

3. **Predominance of Auditory or Visual Errors.** No writer has solely auditory or visual errors. Often, however, the spelling "scale" in dysgraphic writing is tipped quite definitely to one side or the other, suggesting that one of the writer's major spelling routes is seriously dysfunctional. Writers who make mostly auditory errors probably have a dysfunctional visual route; they are categorized as *surface dysgraphics* (the type most commonly found in basic writing classes). Writers who make mostly visual errors probably have a dysfunctional auditory route; they are categorized as *deep dysgraphics.* Some writers, however, may be categorized as both surface and deep dysgraphics, unable to use effectively either the visual or auditory route.

Figure 8 shows the writing of a student diagnosed as a surface dysgraphic, for the errors are mainly auditory. In contrast, the writer of figure 9 was diagnosed as a deep dysgraphic, for the misspellings are mainly visual, due to omitted letters (sounds) both in the middle of words and at the ends. These areas are underlined.

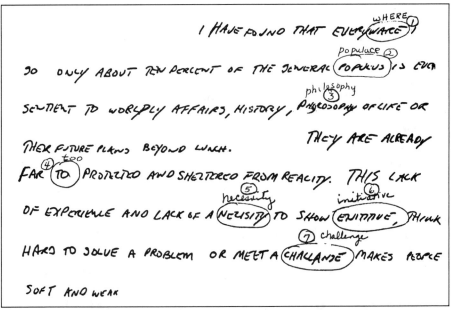

Figure 8. Passage illustrating surface dysgraphia. This passage illustrates many of the characteristics of LD writing—unusual handwriting, confusing syntax, frequent misspellings (several unusual, most of them auditory). The teacher has circled and numbered the spelling errors and written the target word above each error.

Students with such spelling disorders eliminate their errors only with great effort. Figure 10 suggests this effort: the student writer has underlined the words he is unsure of and wants to look up—eight out of eighty-seven words, four correct and four incorrect—and he has missed two spelling errors. The passage indicates how difficult it is for him to *recognize* correctly spelled words by appearance (hence his predominantly auditory errors). The final copy of this essay, however, would not reveal how much time and effort he had put into achieving a ''normal'' level of correct spelling.

Christopher Lee, the student quoted earlier, had the opposite problem: he could not match sounds and letters, so he tried to spell by approximating the appearance of the words. He used an image derived from the handwriting instruction technique of ''boxing'' (drawing boxes around the letters in words) to describe his difficulties with pairing sounds and letters: ''It's as if there are twenty-six letters spinning around in my head, each letter . . . trying to find its own box. . . . I cannot pull the letters down to match . . . these boxes. I have been trying to . . . for

Some day are coplete disasters. On

Wednesday everthing that could go wrong did

go wong. It was a wednes day just like

any other wednesday, nothing was special

about the day and there wasn't anything holding

over from the day befor that would make the

day go bad. The day be fore was nice an everthing

seemed to be alright. I had gotten a good night

sleep the night before, but little did I know

the seris of disaters that I would face that day.

Figure 9. Passage illustrating deep dysgraphia. This passage, transcribed from a handwritten essay, has seven of ten spelling errors caused by missing letters—an indication of the student's inability to relate sounds to spelling. (The areas where letters are missing are underlined.)

almost twenty years." For LD students, writing is indeed often reduced, as Lee says, to a "horizontal spelling test" (Lee and Jackson, 1992, 22–23).

Clearly, it is important for a teacher to be sensitive to poor spellers who may have such learning disabilities. But while teachers should not be too severe with these students ("You get an *F* because you had more than three spelling errors"), they should not go to the other extreme and simply ignore all misspellings. The best route is moderation, and the goal is to teach these students ways to cope with their disabilities.

At the same time, teachers must remember that no matter how consistent and convincing the LD "clues," the psychoeducational evaluation by the team of specialists is the only legal way—and the most reliable way—of determining whether a student should, in fact, be considered learning disabled. Only when the student is officially diagnosed is he or she eligible for special instructional modifications, such

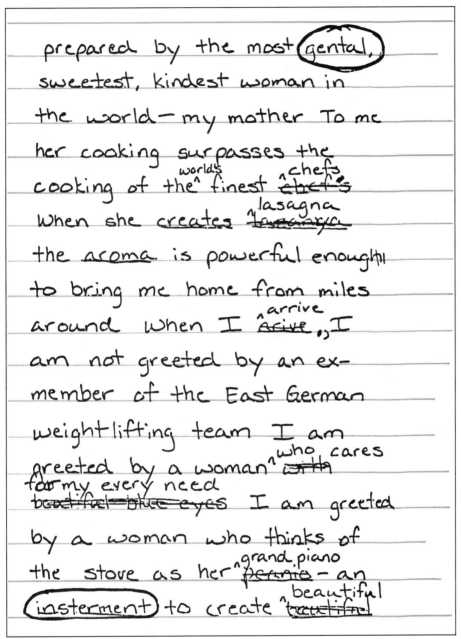

prepared by the most (gental,)
sweetest, kindest woman in
the world — my mother To me
her cooking surpasses the
cooking of the^world's finest ^chefs ~~chef's~~
When she creates ^lasagna ~~lasagna~~
the aroma is powerful enough‖
to bring me home from miles
around when I ^arrive ~~Acive~~,, I
am not greeted by an ex-
member of the East German
weightlifting team I am
greeted by a woman^who ~~with~~ cares
for ^my every need
~~beautiful blue~~ eyes I am greeted
by a woman who thinks of
the stove as her ^grand piano ~~pennio~~ — an
(insterment) to create ^beautiful ~~beautiful~~

Figure 10. Learning disabled student's struggle with spelling. This page from a draft of a student diagnosed as dysgraphic reveals his effort to achieve correct spelling. His errors are auditory, suggesting an ineffective visual route: he cannot judge whether a word is correct by its appearance. Thus he questioned the spelling of eight of his 87 words (which he underlined) and spent time looking them up. Four of those words were indeed misspelled, and he corrected them. He missed two errors, which his teacher has circled.

as the use of word processors for essay tests (when available) and extended time for in-class writing. And while methods for evaluations may vary somewhat from school to school or state to state, such testing is, in general, the most reliable way of defining the specific *nature* of the disability and distinguishing its effects from those of other conditions.

Teachers need to know and follow the policies of their particular school if they suspect that one of their students has a learning disability. However, in most cases, one of the following courses would be appropriate:

1. Consult with the student's counselor or an administrator.
2. Tactfully question the student or parents about any past diagnosis.
3. Suggest to the student's parents (if the student is in high school) or to the student (if the student is in college) that he or she undergo a psychoeducational evaluation to determine if any handicapping conditions (such as learning disabilities) are the cause of the underachievement. Private clinics, most high schools, and many colleges provide such evaluations. Clinics and colleges generally charge a fee. (Contact HEATH for a list of directories of postsecondary centers that identify and offer support to LD students. See References for address.)

Teachers may find that some students (Peter, in the introduction, for example) do not want to be evaluated, or—if the students are in high school—that their parents do not want them to be. Such students or parents may want to deny that there is a problem, or they may fear the stigma of the LD label. Of course, students with less severe disabilities may manage to achieve their academic goals, although often with more than the usual difficulty and stress (some students develop ulcers or succumb to depression) and with lower grades than their efforts would normally deserve. Other students, however, may decide that avoiding evaluation is self-defeating and unrealistic—that to diagnose the problem and begin to deal with it directly and under the guidance of experts is the most constructive course of action. Some, indeed, can succeed only with support and modifications. Usually, any stigma of a label is more than counterbalanced by the students' honesty, motivation, and abilities in other areas.

As we have seen, there may be a number of reasons for the spelling deficiencies of basic writers. Whatever those reasons may be, teachers can employ current research and theory, technology, and an understanding of the English orthographic system to provide most students with effective help. Chapter 2 describes techniques for doing so.

2 Practice

The traditional method of teaching spelling has been that of rote memory during grade school, the underlying assumption being that for most people, spelling skills are easily acquired, probably absorbed through reading in the early years of schooling. Teachers of basic writers at the secondary and postsecondary levels, however, deal with students who, in many cases, have not acquired spelling skills so easily. Some of them, like Dick, have shown little interest in reading and writing; some, like Arthur, lack experience with Standard English; and some, like Charles, have been prevented from absorbing spelling skills because of an auditory or visual processing problem. No wonder that many basic writing teachers, realizing that spelling is important, would like to respond to errors in ways other than de-emphasizing them or lowering grades for too many "sp" labels.

We know, of course, that spelling skills develop concomitantly with increased language experience and maturity, particularly in the context of general language study: students increase their spelling expertise as they read and write. However, research has shown that spelling skills of older students can also be improved with training. In the early 1980s Zephania Davis studied two eighth-grade classes and found that even a basic study-test method of spelling instruction (twenty minutes on Tuesday, test on Thursday) improved skills more than no instruction at all. In a community college in Missouri, the scores of students who took a diagnostic test, studied exercises in a spelling text, and took an equivalent mastery test, improved by an average of 52 percent (Hook, 1986, *vii*). According to research reported in *Toward Better Teaching* (1973), spelling videotapes improved the average student's performance from 76 percent accuracy to 93 percent accuracy (Brown and Pearsall, 1985, *ix*). After teaching her first basic writing class designed for students with spelling problems, Patricia McAlexander noted that the five students whose spelling looked most like that of learning disabled writers had improved, surprisingly, more than the other students. With increased attention to and training in spelling, the number of spelling errors made by these students had, in the last two in-class essays, decreased by more than 50 percent without any decline in the quality of content.

Such information indicates that teachers *can* help poor spellers. Once teachers have diagnosed the spelling-error patterns of their students, they can work to strengthen the spelling routes the students tend to neglect or misapply; and they can teach learning disabled students using dysfunctional routes how to use more effectively the routes that *are* functional—just as one can teach the color-blind to read traffic signals not by making them "see red," but by teaching them that the red light is at the top of the signal.

Preliminary Activities

Planning Spelling Instruction

First, teachers must determine whether there is a need to include a formal spelling component within their composition curriculum. As teachers read student papers, they can bear in mind various options regarding the teaching of spelling. If the writing class consists of students with only minor spelling problems, the teacher will probably want simply to interweave spelling instruction informally into the curriculum, along with vocabulary, reading skills, and essay writing. The students with one or two weak areas may be tutored on an individual basis. In schools fortunate enough to have writing centers or labs (found mostly at the postsecondary level), teachers can send these students to such facilities for tutoring.

However, in basic writing classes, a large number of students often exhibit moderate to severe spelling problems (five to ten errors per hundred words). We recommend that when a composition class has a significant number of such poor spellers, a series of spelling lessons be incorporated into the curriculum. Not only is such instruction a more natural way to teach a language skill, but it also tends to be more effective than other, more specialized means of instruction. Some schools offer elective credit or noncredit courses in spelling only (e.g., McClellan, 1978, describes a voluntary "Spelling Clinic" she set up at her college), but while such classes and clinics may be successful, they often attract only a small percentage of students with spelling problems. Moreover, group or individual tutoring by classroom teachers or writing center instructors can be limited by time constraints. Students have concerns about more immediate course requirements, and classroom teachers, unfortunately, often have too many classes and too heavy student loads to have time for extended tutoring in a specialized area.

If teachers thus do decide to incorporate spelling lessons into their course, they must determine how much time to take from their class schedule. Luckily, the amount of time needed, according to most of the research, is not much. A number of studies from the 1950s and '60s, although dealing mostly with presecondary levels, indicate that it is more efficient "to involve students in a highly motivated spelling experience for a short period of time than it is to involve them in successive, lengthy daily experience of study and practice" (Allred, 1977, 33). For example, Oscar T. Jarvis (1963) found that children in the intermediate grades benefited as much from a twenty-minute spelling period each day as they did from a forty-minute period. The explanation seems simple: shorter periods better sustain interest and motivation.

Current literature on the teaching of spelling for secondary and postsecondary levels concurs. Ann Dobie suggests a plan for a "short course in spelling," using fifteen to twenty minutes of each fifty-minute class three times a week (in a three-day-per-week, fifteen-week course) for three to four weeks. McAlexander, Gregg, and Winger developed a similar plan for a ten-week, quarter-system course designed specifically for weak spellers in the University of Georgia Developmental Studies program. One section of composition per ten-week quarter was set aside for these students when it was needed; in a five-day week, spelling instruction was given for about thirty minutes, two days a week. The students for the first-quarter course were identified on the basis of their placement essay; for second- and third-quarter courses, on the basis of faculty recommendations. (Another option is simply to allow interested students to register for these "spelling" sections of composition.)

The McAlexander-Gregg-Winger curriculum focused on spelling problems shared by a majority of the students in the class. Students with additional problems not related to the class lessons were given individual tutoring sessions by the instructor. Because this tutoring was integrated with the coursework and because, as a supplement to the course, it required relatively little time, students successfully completed the individualized sequences. See figure 11 for a week-by-week schedule of possible spelling activities in such a composition class.

Motivating the Students

One of the teacher's first tasks, even in a very short course on spelling, is to motivate the students. Student attitudes toward spelling vary greatly. Many students already realize its importance, struggle with the spelling problems they know they have, and even insist on their desire to be independent of (or to avoid) technology such as word processors' spell checks. Others simply dismiss the problem ("Spelling isn't important") or plan to rely on others ("Someday I'll have a secretary") or

Possible Schedule of Spelling Lessons for a Composition Class
(10-week quarter)

Week 1.   Diagnostic essay
Introductory lecture on error types
Individual conferences

Week 2.   Rule 1: *i* before *e*

Week 3.   Rule 2: vowel length with silent *e*
Rule 3: adding suffixes that begin with vowels to words ending in silent *e*
Rule 4: adding suffixes that begin with vowels to words ending in a single conso-
nant—optional)

Week 4.   Rule 5: adding suffixes that begin with a consonant
Rule 6: adding suffixes to words ending in *y*

Week 5.   Problem Area 2: pronunciation and spelling mismatches
Problem Area 3: unstressed vowels

Week 6.   Problem Area 5: homonyms

Week 7.   Unit on dictionary and word elements

Week 8.   Week 8. Problem Area 1: compound, segmented, and hyphenated words

Week 9.   Rule 7: forming plurals
Rule 8: apostrophes

Week 10. Review

Throughout the course: Individual spelling lists and rules
Practice with word processors/spell checks
Practice with electronic spellers
Exercises and tests

Figure 11. Sample spelling course schedule. Individual teachers, of course, tailor their schedules to the needs of the class. The rule and problem-area numbers above refer to sections in this book.

on technology ("I'll just use a computer to write"). And some, of course, externalize the blame for their spelling weaknesses, complaining that the fault lies not in themselves but in the spelling system ("English spelling is crazy") and expressing the wish that everyone could just spell words the way they sound.

Teachers thus may find it useful to begin their course on spelling by responding to these points. They may give a pep talk about self-reliance. (Secretaries can't always spell correctly. Often, individuals will have to write their own letters without the help of a secretary or a computer. Checking a large number of misspellings on a computer can be very time-consuming.) Conversely, teachers may need to talk about the importance of being willing to use technology when it is available. As for the difficulty of English spelling, certainly teachers can sympathize and agree (and perhaps give the students some background on other spelling systems and the development of English orthography, as described in chapter 1). To illustrate the problems with individual phonetic spelling, however, teachers can show the class a passage from one of the nineteenth-century, local-color "dialect" tales which carry this kind of spelling to such an extreme that the works are often almost impossible to read for any sustained length of time. (See p. 8 for such an excerpt). The difficulty of reading such passages usually silences students' complaints about the illogic and rigidity of English spelling.

In addition to addressing the initial objections of students, teachers will want to point out the importance of correct spelling. They can quote or give their version of Mina Shaughnessy's statement that "the ability to spell is viewed by many as one of the marks of an educated person, and the failure of a college graduate to meet that minimal standard of advanced literacy is cause to question the quality of his education or even his intelligence" (1977, 161–62). Teachers can usually come up with personal stories to illustrate this second point, stories like the one Ann Dobie (1986) recounts of the university committee that turned down an outstanding candidate because of three misspelled words in the applicant's own letter. Figure 12 humorously suggests the negative impact spelling errors have—even on students.

Teachers might also want to describe the 1981 survey of personnel officers in the 500 largest corporations in the United States to determine preferences in job application letters and personal résumés. Of the fifty-one items under consideration, good grammar and spelling were rated highest (Brown and Pearsall, 1985, *vii*). Combined with this talk about the importance of correct spelling, of course, should be the point that, with effort, spelling usually can be improved. As John Irving points out in his essay "How to Spell" (1983), 90 percent of all writing consists of 1,000 basic words.

Teacher Jim Hahn describes another method for raising students' motivation, one that is mainly applicable to high school students: he talks with each student individually and "if a student does not want to improve her spelling, . . . I ask her to write a short letter to her parents explaining [that fact], . . . take it home and get it signed." Sometimes, he says, the student returns without the letter and declares a change of heart (1990, 7).

But perhaps the most successful activity for motivating students is to analyze each student's spelling error patterns. Doing so not only raises the student's interest in spelling, but also suggests a plan for improvement. The specific strengths and weaknesses indicated by the

Figure 12. Cartoon. This cartoon suggests the effects of misspelling on readers—even students. Originally in the *Phi Delta Kappan,* May 1988, 638. (Reprinted by permission from James K. Warren, cartoonist.)

analysis can serve as building blocks for the teacher's approach to the classes or to individual students.

Analyzing Student Spelling Errors

Diagnostic tests, included in many spelling textbooks (e.g., *Better Spelling*), often can be helpful in analyzing the errors students make. Even better (because it is more realistic) is the diagnostic essay. An essay that is written spontaneously—in class, with no peer review and no specific time set aside for proofreading—will provide the best sample of errors. Another diagnostic resource is the journal entry, particularly when students know they are not being graded on spelling. Figure 13 shows lists of individual student spelling errors taken from ninth graders' journals over a three-month period.

As the teacher reads the student writing (whatever its nature), not only during this preliminary analysis period but also throughout the spelling course, his or her highlighting or listing of each spelling error is helpful.

Analysis of a student's errors begins with a spelling error frequency count (i.e., the number of misspellings per 100 words). A student with ten or more errors per 100 words has a severe spelling problem; five out of 100 errors indicates a moderate problem. The errors should then be classified according to the error types categorized in chapter 1. If an

Student 1

an (for *and*)
ocation
strenuos
fimiliar
aquainting
knew (for *new*)
recieve
discribe
incourage
symbolizum
its (for *it's*)
succed
exceptable (for *acceptable*)
refering
resite
permitt
aggrevate
curtisy
recomend
intail

Student 2

dureing
expieriences
extremly
writeing
finaly
actualy
useing
piont (for *point*)
choseing
writen
oppisite
latter (for *later*)
apsolutely
piza
dilivery
littel
crys
dicided
acksadentally
niether
Colobus day
niehborhood
liveing
athority
alot
whose (for *who's*)
to much
pioson (for *poison*)

Student 3

lagg
corse
eairly
allerges
begining
secreat
board (for *bored*)
offically
rehersal
supprised
incouraged
moutian
acidemicle
arn't suposed
entrys
stincks

Student 4

usualy
assingment
latter on
rememberd
charicters
notic (for *notice*)
eals (for *else*)
personaly
straped
remanes
storys
gramer

Student 5

whats
thats
would of
emotionaly
its (for *it's*)

Student 6

drasticly
forrest
assasinated
reciever

Student 7

forrest
gravle
takeing
realy
tottaly
promice
probibly
wrighting (for *writing*)
advantag
ammount
alot
tireing
english
familliar
wate
concerne
peacefull
falt
allmost
thir (for *their*)
insid
exept
painfuly
bucketts
finaly
doesnt
exighted (for *excited*)
offon (for *often*)
privilage
finnished
suspission
personaly
parragraph
usuialy
describtive
responce
barley (for *barely*)
studing
credid (for *credit*)
yesturday
live (for *life*)
racisum

Student 8

No misspelled words.

Figure 13. Individual error lists from ninth graders' journal entries. These lists of errors were gathered over a three-month period by the students' English teacher. (Courtesy Janet M. Goldstein, teacher of upper school English, Friends Select School, Philadelphia, Pennsylvania.)

error is ambiguous—that is, if it can fit into more than one category—it should be affixed with all applicable labels. There will, of course, always be the student who makes a hodgepodge of errors, but, as we noted earlier, the misspellings of most students fall into patterns that suggest where the students' major weakness or weaknesses lie. Figure 14 shows a spelling error analysis of a passage with mainly auditory errors, suggesting a visual-processing weakness in the writer. Figure 15 shows a spelling error analysis of a passage where visual errors dominate, indicating that the writer has an auditory-processing weakness. The number of errors at the ends of words might also suggest a lack of experience with Standard Written English.

For accuracy of analysis, it is necessary for the *teacher* to make the preliminary error count and classification; however, many educators point out the benefits of student participation in this process. An inductive (if possible) lecture/discussion centering on spelling routes and error types (pp. 13–18), followed by the students' analyzing their own errors—perhaps in photocopies of the diagnostic essay or in later essays, or in personal error lists—will raise their awareness of their own spelling strengths and weaknesses. It is particularly effective for the teacher to ask the students how they determine a word's spelling. Students are surprisingly knowledgeable about the methods they use, and thus their error types will usually be easy for them to discover.

Whether or not their writing classes include specific instruction in spelling, teachers may want to give their students a "spelling survey" like that designed by Kristine F. Anderson (1987) to help students develop a greater awareness of their spelling strategies and weaknesses. The survey—a checklist answered by "Always," "Frequently," "Occasionally," or "Never"—asks questions about spelling strategies, proofreading or editing, and the student's error patterns. (See figure 16.)

In conferences, teacher and student can go over the analyses of the diagnostic materials and make a tentative diagnosis about routes that the student needs to strengthen. An accurate sense of doubt is very important in spelling, and if students realize that they have problems with a particular type (or types) of error, they will be more likely to check the spelling of words in that category. Self-awareness alone will often lead weak spellers to improve. The writer of the passage in figure 14, for example, can learn that nearly all her errors are auditory, with several semantic (homonym) errors. Because these patterns suggest a visual weakness, she needs to strengthen her visual acuity and awareness (techniques for doing so are listed later in this chapter), use

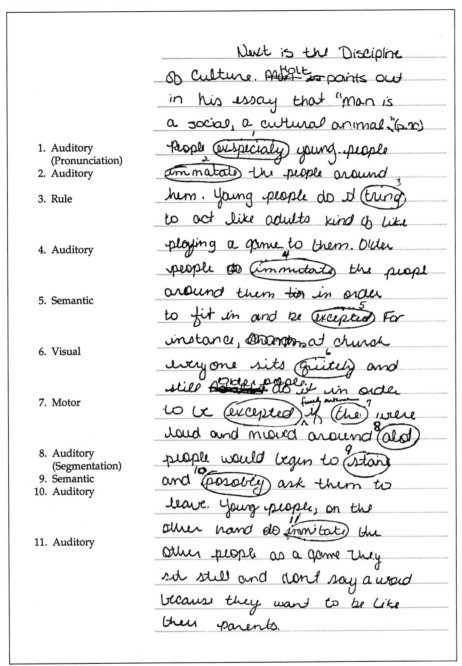

1. Auditory (Pronunciation)
2. Auditory
3. Rule
4. Auditory
5. Semantic
6. Visual
7. Motor
8. Auditory (Segmentation)
9. Semantic
10. Auditory
11. Auditory

Figure 14. Sample analysis of spelling error types (indicates visual-processing weakness). The teacher has circled the errors; the error types are listed in the left margin. Five of the eleven errors are auditory, suggesting a visual-processing weakness. The two homonym (semantic) errors are a form of auditory error. (The repeated error—*excepted*—is not counted the second time.)

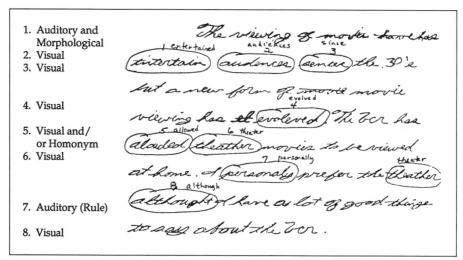

Figure 15. Sample analysis of spelling error types (indicates auditory-processing weakness). Of the eight different spelling errors made in 45 words (circled, with target word written above), six are visual errors. This pattern indicates an auditory-processing weakness. The word-ending errors might suggest a lack of experience with Standard English—and perhaps overcorrection—or a motor problem.

supplemental routes (particularly the semantic route, which involves awareness of homonyms), and work with individual word lists.

A second classification teachers should make as they analyze the students' diagnostic essays involves noting whether the misspellings are typical errors—those found often in the writing of their particular population of students—or unusual errors. Of course, the "typicality" of a particular error will vary. A misspelling common to Hispanic students in Texas may be rarely found in a group of students of German heritage in Minnesota—and vice versa. Figure 17 shows how one teacher classified some errors of her students at the University of Georgia.

Whatever the nature of a teacher's students, a writer making an inordinately high number of misspellings, particularly rarely found misspellings, may have a learning disability. Especially if other LD "symptoms" are present, the teacher should consider referring such students for psychoeducational evaluation. The writers of the passages in figures 14 and 15 were both advised to undergo such evaluation, the first because of the frequency of her misspellings, the second because his spelling errors were not only frequent but, in his teacher's opinion, unusual. In figure 13, the ninth graders' lists of individual errors, the atypical misspellings of students 2 and 7 indicate possible learning disabilities. Interestingly, the one student in that ninth-grade class who

Individual Spelling Survey				
Kristine F. Anderson Southern College of Technology Marietta, Georgia	Always	Frequently	Occasionally	Never

1. Do you try to spell words the way you think they sound?

2. Do you try to use spelling rules when appropriate?

3. If you cannot spell a word, do you consider the meaning or structure of the word?

4. If you cannot spell a word, do you consider the spelling of a related word or a word in the same family?

5. Do you use a dictionary or wordbook rather than a thesaurus?

6. Can you tell if a word you've written doesn't "look right"?

7. Do you take time to proofread specifically for spelling errors as you write?

8. Do you take time to proofread specifically for spelling errors as you edit?

9. a. Do you keep a current list of misspelled words?

   b. Do you frequently misspell the same words?

10. Do you notice any pattern in your misspelled words?

    a. Words with silent letters

    b. Words with unstressed vowels—schwa [ə]

    c. Words with prefixes

    d. Words with suffixes

    e. Words with a Latin or Greek root

    f. Homonym forms

    g. Common words and phrases, including transitions

    h. Miscellaneous

Figure 16. Anderson's spelling survey. An earlier version was published in *Journal of Basic Writing* 6 (1987): 77. (Courtesy Kristine F. Anderson, professor of English and reading, Southern College of Technology, Marietta, Georgia.)

Misspelled Words	Target Word	Typical (T) or Unusual (U)
intrest	interest	T
whith	with	U
compareing	comparing	U
cocach	coach	U
She staired at me.	stared	U
use to	used to	T
highschool	high school	T
sociolog	sociology	U
wich	which	T

Figure 17. Spelling errors classified as unusual or typical. There is no absolute answer as to whether a misspelling is unusual or typical. A teacher's classification reflects the students he or she teaches, their backgrounds, and the region of the country they live in. The misspellings above labeled "U" were found infrequently in one particular teacher's student population (at the University of Georgia).

had not misspelled anything in her journal, even after several months, was an avid reader, suggesting again the connection often found between wide reading and good spelling, provided there is no cognitive dysfunction.

Keeping Track of Student Spelling Errors

Throughout the spelling course, students should continue to keep track of their errors and note their individual misspelling patterns. Teachers can determine a method for doing so that will suit their own teaching style as well as the learning styles of their students. There are a number of different types of charts that stress different aspects of instruction. Chart 1 (figure 18), for example, stresses the individual words that are misspelled: the students list the correct version of each misspelled word and label the error type or problem area it illustrates.

Chart 2 (figure 19) records only error types, simply keeping a checklist of the number of times a student made certain categories of errors.

A third method (figure 20) is to have students write the correct spelling of each misspelled word on a 3" x 5" index card, along with its pronunciation and a sentence using the word (Sharknas, 1970). An advantage of index cards is that they can be alphabetized and used as

INDIVIDUAL SPELLING LIST

This list is one of the most important elements of the course.
Keep track of words that you misspell--not every single one, but
ones that you know you will use again and again. I will include
some of your personal words on spelling quizzes from now on. Also
we will check the list to see if the lessons we do in class apply
to them.

WORD (spelled correctly)	Essay #	Rule/Problem Area
victim	1	Problem Area 3
receiving	1	Rule 1
incredible	1	Rule 10
cockiness	2	Rule 6
handful	2	Word Elements (VII)
arrogance	2	Problem Area 3
baking	3	Rule 3
surprised	3	Problem Area 2

Figure 18. Sample spelling chart 1. This type of chart stresses specific words the
student has misspelled. The word, spelled correctly, appears in column 1; the essay in
which the error appeared is listed in column 2; the rule or problem area (here, numbered
to correspond with this book's "lessons" or sections) is listed in column 3. Some
teachers might want to include the word as it was misspelled in an additional, far-left
column.

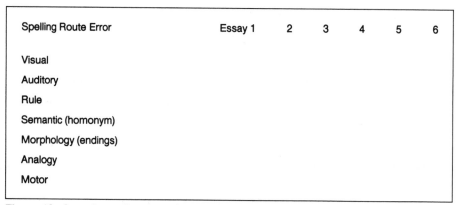

Spelling Route Error	Essay 1	2	3	4	5	6
Visual						
Auditory						
Rule						
Semantic (homonym)						
Morphology (endings)						
Analogy						
Motor						

Figure 19. Sample spelling chart 2. This chart is designed to raise the student's awareness of weak areas in general, and not of specific errors. At a glance, the student can see areas of improvement and areas needing continued work. (Adapted from Meyer, Pisha, Rose, "Process and Product in Writing: Computer as Enabler," in *Written Language Disorders,* 1991, 123.)

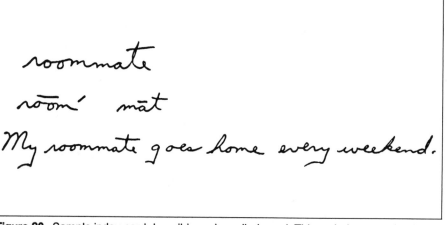

Figure 20. Sample index card describing misspelled word. This technique emphasizes individual words. An advantage of index cards is that they can be alphabetized and used as a personal dictionary.

a personal dictionary. Or, students might simply list words they have misspelled on one 4" x 6" card (Buck, 1977).

To enhance visual awareness, whenever the students write their misspelled words on one of these charts or lists, they might use Norman Hall's Letter Mark-Out System (1962): They write the word as they misspelled it, then mark out any letter or letters missed in the word, write the correct letter or letters (if any) above the marked-out ones, and then rewrite the complete word to the side of the original spelling. This method focuses attention on the parts of the word that they misspelled. Hence,

visᵢble   visible

Forming a Spelling Error "Bank"

Teachers may wish to make a periodic check of the students' record-keeping and record for themselves some of the most common spelling errors. Since students at a particular school and at particular levels often use the same vocabulary and make the same spelling errors, these errors can be used as a bank from which to draw illustrations for the spelling lessons. Students will be more motivated if they realize the lessons apply to words they really use. Such banks also indicate which spelling lessons would be of most value to the school's particular population. Some English departments, in fact, use such error banks to form a departmental spelling list which the students must master. For an example of such a list, see figure 21.

These preliminary activities—discussing spelling, analyzing student errors, and setting up a method for keeping track of errors—will probably take at least the first week of spelling instruction time. After this point, however, most of the students should be receptive to instruction designed to help them improve their spelling.

In the following pages, we present information that teachers can use in such instruction, whether for a whole class or for an individual, whether for spontaneous lessons inserted into the regular composition curriculum or for more systematic, regularly scheduled spelling instruction. We begin with a number of spelling lessons which cover rules and problem areas in English spelling. Next are sections on mnemonic devices and techniques and exercises to strengthen the major spelling routes. Then we describe language arts units—on the dictionary and word elements—that can improve spelling. Of course, we describe some spelling tests—tests that teach as well as evaluate. Finally, we have sections on proofreading techniques and technical aids that all poor spellers should learn to use.

English Spelling Rules

For centuries rhymes and sayings have helped students remember spelling rules, and linguistic studies of recent decades have demonstrated predictable patterns in English spelling. In 1963, for example, Paul Hanna and a team of researchers at Stanford University analyzed 17,310

Words Frequently Confused

accept, except	later, latter
advice, advise	lead, led
affect, effect	lightning, lightening
already, all ready	lose, loose
altar, alter	maybe, may be
always, all ways	minor, miner
angel, angle	moral, morale
bare, bear	of, off
breath, breathe	passed, past
choose, chose	peace, piece
site, cite, sight	principle, principal
clothes, cloths	prophecy, prophesy
conscience, conscious	quiet, quite, quit
desert, dessert	sense, since
device, devise	than, then
formally, formerly	their, there, they're
forth, fourth	through, thorough
hear, here	to, too, two
heard, herd	weather, whether
hole, whole	were, where
its, it's	who's, whose
your, you're	

Words Frequently Misspelled

all right	occurred
a lot of	opportunity
among	privilege
athletics	probably
believe	really
certain	receive
chief	recognize
chosen	recommend
Christian	restaurant
definitely	separate
different	similar
especially	skiing
familiar	sophomore
forty	stopped
government	strength
grammar	studying
guard	surprise
guidance	tragedy
heroes	truly
interest	undoubtedly
meant	until
necessary	view

Figure 21. Gainesville College departmental spelling list. Some English departments draw on the most common student spelling errors to form a spelling list which students must master. (Courtesy Gainesville College English faculty, Georgia.)

words from the "common core" vocabulary and determined that English spelling *is* basically regular/systematic, with sound-spelling correspondences determined by adjacent sounds and letters. Further emphasizing regularity in English spelling, Richard Venezky (1967) pointed out that words with common roots have related spellings despite sound changes—as seen in *sane* and *sanity; nation* and *national; derive, derivation,* and *derivative.* And in 1971, after further research, Hanna, Hodges, and Hanna concluded, "About half of the words in ordinary speech can be spelled correctly by the application of principles based on the alphabetic nature of American-English orthography. And most of the remaining words can be spelled correctly if one couples a knowledge of sound-letter correspondences with a knowledge of the characteristic word-building and word-borrowing patterns of our language" (96).

Thus, to begin their series of spelling lessons, teachers may wish to present their classes with particular rules—generalizations about the order or pattern of letters in particular categories of English words. With a rule, instead of learning to spell the long way—memorizing one word at a time—students can immediately be able to spell a large number of words. Some educators, of course, are skeptical of such rules. They argue that rules are prescriptive, while the best form of teaching is inductive; that there are too many exceptions to rules; and that many students cannot understand, remember, or apply rules.

It is true that students with good memories, reading comprehension, and visual and auditory skills can best implement spelling rules. Ironically, these are the students who usually are good spellers anyway. But weak spellers, who have the greatest need for these rules as an alternate route to correct spelling, can employ at least some of them. We have seen many students eliminate large numbers of errors just on the basis of learning one or two simple rules.

Many of the problems with rules can be eliminated if the teacher follows Thomas Foran's "rules about rules" (1934, 144–47), summarized below:

   a. Teach only a few rules, and only those that have few or no exceptions.

   b. Teach rules inductively and integrate them with groups of words.

   c. Teach only one rule at a time.

   d. Teach a rule only when there is a need for it.

   e. Review rules frequently.

f. Focus on the student's ability to use rules, not simply quote them.

We would like to add three more rules to Foran's:

g. State the rule as simply as possible. (Some rules sound so complicated that the students are discouraged before they begin. It helps when a teacher can "translate" the rules and devise techniques to help the students remember the pattern.)

h. Try to have one rule build on another, in a logical order.

i. Use as illustrations words frequently used by the students.

We try to follow all these "rules about rules" in our descriptions below. Rules 1–9 are major rules that are usually worth teaching to entire classes. Rules 10–21 are minor ones usually best employed only to help individuals who have problems with those particular patterns. The minor rules are in alphabetical order according to the letter(s) being discussed.

Rule 1: *i* before *e*

This is a good rule to begin a spelling course with because it illustrates to students how rules ideally should work. It is a grade-school favorite, one students will probably remember; it is simple; it has few exceptions; and it applies to over 1,000 common words.

The rule, of course, reads like this:

i before *e*
except after *c*
or when sounded like *a*
as in *neighbor* or *weigh*.

The most frequently misspelled word that can be corrected by this rule is *receive*. In fact, teachers are usually pleasantly surprised when students spell that word correctly.

Exceptions

1. Remind the students that this rule applies only when the *ei* or *ie* letters represent one sound—either the long *e* or the long *a*. It does not apply to two syllables, as in the word *society*.
2. Common exceptions to this rule are found in the following sentence: The *ancient* man in a *foreign* land *seized their* hands.
3. Other common exceptions to memorize are *either, neither, weird,* and *leisure*.

Overall, however, the "i before e" rule is one of the safest to follow.

Rule 2: Vowel Length with Silent *e*

Usually in a word ending in a final silent *e* (the *e* itself is not pronounced), the preceding vowel is long (*pine*). Drop the *e* and the vowel becomes short (*pin*).

This rule enables a student to know when to add the silent *e* to a one-syllable word and when to leave it off. (I *mop* the floor when it's dirty; I *mope* when I feel depressed. The angry dog gave me a *scare*; Tom showed me the *scar* from his injury.)

Exceptions

The words *come* and *some* have short vowels even though they end in a silent *e*.

Rule 3: Adding Suffixes That Begin with Vowels to Words Ending in Silent *e*

If a word ends in silent *e*, DROP that *e* when you add a suffix beginning with a vowel:

pine + ing = pining

pine + ed = pined (that *e* comes from the suffix)

scare + ing = scaring

scare + ed = scared

advise + able = advisable

With this rule, students should never write about eating in *dinning rooms*, *metting* new people, or *writting* essays again. They should remember, however, that when adding *-ing* to *come*, even though the vowel is short, they should follow the pattern of words ending in silent *e*: the correct spelling is *coming*, not *comming*.

Exception

The silent *e* is retained if the *c* or *g* preceding it is soft (pronounced as *s* or *j*) as in *peaceable* and *manageable*.

Rule 4: Adding Suffixes That Begin with Vowels to Words Ending in a Single Consonant

For one-syllable words that have short vowels and no silent *e*, *double* the final consonant before adding a suffix that begins with a vowel:

pin + ing = pinning

pin + ed = pinned

scar + ed = scarred

Eileen Stirling (1989) uses an analogy illustrated in figure 22 to help her students remember this rule: She pictures the short or weak vowel as living in a castle; being weak, its castle needs two "walls" (or consonants) to keep it from being "invaded" and transformed into a long vowel when a suffix is added.

However, the doubling does not always apply to words of more than one syllable. Then we have another, broader rule to follow, represented by the following pattern, in which C = a consonant and V = a vowel:

$$CVC + V$$

What the pattern means: When adding an ending that begins with a vowel (+V) to a word that has its last syllable accented (accent mark) and that ends in a consonant-vowel-consonant pattern (CVC), DOUBLE the final consonant.

Examples: begín + ing = beginning

omít + ed = omitted

If, however, just ONE part of the pattern does not fit, do NOT double the final consonant. SAY the word to determine where the accent is. This rule is particularly helpful when endings like *-ed* and *-ing* are added to verbs because dictionaries do not always include all forms of every verb. Example of the CV́C + V rule:

éxit + ed = exited

Exceptions

1. *Transfer* (he requested a transfer): the *r* is doubled even though the accent is on the FIRST (not last) syllable: he transferred to another school.
2. Some words can be spelled with *either* a single or double consonant. Examples: *traveller* or *traveler, focused* or *focussed*. (Note: Some students find it difficult to determine where the accent is and so have trouble applying the rule. If this is the case, rather than frustrate them, move on. The simpler "doubling the consonant rule" can be applied with many words they use.)

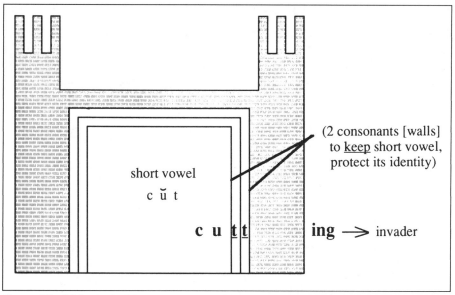

Figure 22. Stirling's doubling rule analogy. Stirling tells her students to imagine the short or weak vowel as living in a castle. Being weak, its castle needs two "walls" (consonants) to keep it from being "invaded" and transformed into a long vowel when a suffix is added. ("The Adolescent Dyslexic: Strategies for Spelling," *Annals of Dyslexia* 39 [1989]: 271–72.) (Graphics by Keri Turner.)

Rule 5: Adding Suffixes That Begin with a Consonant

Usually, when adding suffixes that begin with a consonant, simply add the suffix. Retain all letters. This rule is particularly important for forming adverbs by adding *-ly* to an adjective:

complete + ly = completely

quick + ly = quickly

Students often want to omit one *l* when adding *ly* to a word that ends in *l*. This rule should stop them from that error, so that they will not write *generaly, finaly, mentaly,* or *physicaly* again.

Exceptions

1. When adding *ly* to words that end in *-ic*, add an *al* before the *-ly: automatically, drastically, tragically.* The exception to this exception is *publicly.*
2. When adding a suffix beginning with a consonant to words ending in *ue*, the final *e* is dropped: *argument, truly.*
3. Words ending in consonant plus *y*. (See rule 6.)

Rule 6: Adding Suffixes to Words Ending in *y*

When a word ends in a consonant plus *y*, to add any suffix except those beginning with *i*, change the *y* to *i*: *cry + ed = cried*. If the suffix begins with *i*, leave the *y* to avoid having two *i*'s together. (The only time two *i*'s appear together in English is with a Scandinavian word—*skiing*.) Examples:

> try + ed = tried
> funny + er = funnier
> try + ing = trying
> fancy + ful = fanciful
> happy + ness = happiness

With this rule, students should never be *studing*—or *studiing*—(or *tring* to study) hard for a test again.

Exceptions

1. If the suffix is just an *-s* (as for plurals and third-person, present-tense verbs), students may well remember the childhood chant, "Change *y* to *i* and add *es*." Examples:

> try + s = tries
> ally + s = allies

2. When the word ends in a *vowel* plus *y*, keep the *y* when adding endings. Examples:

> monkey + s = monkeys
> attorney + s = attorneys

Exception: money + s = monies

Rule 7: Forming Plurals

Most English words are made plural just by adding the letter *s* (*sweater, sweaters*).

Exceptions

1. When a word ends in a consonant plus *y*, change the *y* to *i* and add *es*. (See rule 6.)
2. Some words that end in a consonant plus *o* add *-es* (*hero, heroes; zero, zeroes*).
3. When s is added to words ending in a single *f*, the *f* is often changed to *v* and *-es* is added (*self, selves; half, halves; wife, wives*).

4. When words end in sibilants (hissing sounds)—*ch, sh, x,* and *z*—add *-es* (*Christmases, taxes*).

5. English has a number of irregular plurals, such as *foot/feet*. However, most students know these; the most common confusion is *woman, women* because the two words are pronounced so similarly.

6. Some common borrowed plurals are also irregular. Often, words that end in *-us* are pluralized by changing *us* to *i* (*alumnus, alumni; syllabus, syllabi*). Words ending in *-um* are pluralized by changing the *um* to *a* (*bacterium, bacteria*). Words ending in *-a* are pluralized by changing *a* to *ae* (*vertebra, vertebrae*). Sometimes, however, an alternate form of the plural of such words is formed by simply following the English rules above (e.g., *syllabuses*).

Rule 8: Apostrophes

Apostrophes are used as follows:

In Contractions. Contractions are combinations of two words formed by omitting a letter or letters. The apostrophe indicates the omission:

> I am = I'm
> he is = he's
> will not = won't

In Possessives. An apostrophe + *s* forms the possessive of most singular nouns and plural nouns not ending in *s*:

> Tom's hat is red.
> The women's group met regularly.

For plural nouns ending in *s*, add only the apostrophe:

> The boys' hats were red.

For singular nouns ending in *s*, if the added *'s* results in an awkward *s* sound, add only the apostrophe. Pronunciations of such words, however, may vary. The extra *s* syllable should be added if one pronounces it.

> Dr. Hayes' class *or* Dr. Hayes's class.

Note 1: Do not add an apostrophe to the possessive case of a personal pronoun such as *its*. The meaning of *it's* is *it is*.

Note 2: The possessive case is used not only for literal ownership but in any situation where an *of* phrase can be used. Thus an apostrophe should be used in such phrases as *today's world* (*the world of today*).

In Plurals of Numbers, Letters, and Words Used as Terms. Use an apostrophe, for example, as follows:

> His 7's were hard to read.
>
> He pronounced his *s*'s strangely.

Rule 9: Hyphens in Compound Adjectives and with Prefixes

Hyphens in Compound Words Used as Adjectives. When writers use two or more usually separate words as one adjective before a noun, those words should be hyphenated: *sixteen-year-old boy, six-cylinder engine, computer-assisted course.* This practice also eliminates the possibility of misreading: instead of having a *black, skinned turtle,* we have a *black-skinned turtle.*

Hyphens with Prefixes. When the prefixes *all-, ex-,* and *self-* are attached to words, use hyphens *(all-inclusive, ex-wife, self-confidence).* Also, use a hyphen before a capital letter *(un-American),* before a similar vowel *(re-establish),* or in a compound word *(anti-gun control).*

Rule 10: *-able* versus *-ible*

Add *-able* to (1) full words: *adapt, adaptable; work, workable;* (2) words that end in a single *e*—but drop the *e: love, lovable;* (3) words that end in two *e*'s—but keep both *e*'s: *agree, agreeable; foresee, foreseeable.*

Add *-ible* to (1) a root or base that cannot stand on its own as a word: *credible, tangible, terrible;* (2) to words that end in a soft *c (s)* sound (drop the final *e*): *force, forcible;* (3) to root words ending in *-ns: responsible* (warn students that the root is not *respond,* but *respons-*); and (4) to root words ending in *-miss: permissible.*

Rule 11: *-ary* versus *-ery*

When a word has its major (primary) accent on the first syllable and a less heavy (secondary) accent on the next-to-last syllable (séc re tár y, míl i tár y), it usually ends in *-ary.*

Exceptions

Four words like this end in *-ery: cemetery, millinery, monastery,* and *stationery* (as in letter paper).

Students might try writing and memorizing a sentence that includes these words in order to remember these exceptions.

Example: On the way to the *monastery cemetery,* the *millinery* worker stopped by the *stationery* shop for notepaper to write a note to the bereaved.

Rule 12: *-cede* or *-ceed*—the Final "Seed" Sound

Most words ending in the "seed" sound are spelled *-cede: concede, precede, recede* (from the Latin *cedere,* to withdraw or yield).

Exceptions

Three are spelled *-ceed;* remember them in this sentence: *Proceed, exceed* your rivals, and you will *succeed.*

One word is spelled *-sede: supersede.*

Rule 13: The Final *ch* Sound

When the "ch" sound is at the end of a one-syllable word and is preceded by a short vowel, it is usually spelled *-tch (match, stitch).* When prefixes or suffixes are attached to these one-syllable words, the spelling remains the same *(mismatch).*

When the word has more than one syllable *(sandwich)* or when the preceding vowel sound is long *(reach),* the spelling is *-ch. Exceptions:* Some common words, such as *such, much,* and *kitchen* are exceptions.

Rule 14: *-efy* versus *-ify*

Only four words end in *-efy: stupefy, liquefy, putrefy, rarefy.* Furthermore, most dictionaries list *-ify* as an alternate spelling for all but *putrefy,* so students might as well simply remember to use *-ify.*

Rule 15: The Final *f* Sound

The final *f* sound is usually spelled *ff* when preceded by a short single-lettered vowel *(staff, stiff, scoff, stuff).* When the short vowel sound is formed by *au* or *ou,* the spelling is usually *gh (enough, laugh, rough).*

Rule 16: The *im-* versus *in-* Prefix

The *im-* prefix rather than *in-* is used before the letters *b, m,* and *p* *(imbibe, immodest, impatient).*

Rule 17: *-ize* versus *-ise*

Most words ending with the *-ize* sound are spelled *-ize* when they are formed from a complete word: *item, itemize; apology, apologize.* When the sound follows the letter *v* or is added to an incomplete word, use *-ise: advise, surprise, advertise.*

Exceptions

Only two words have still a different way of spelling that sound: *analyze* and *paralyze*.

Rule 18: Final *j* Sound

The final *j* sound is usually spelled *-dge* when preceded by a short vowel *(ridge, ledge)* and *-ge* when preceded by a long vowel *(age, siege)*.

Rule 19: The Initial *k* Sound

The initial *k* sound is usually spelled *k* when followed by the vowel *i* or *e (kitchen, kettle)*. It is usually spelled *c* when followed by *a, o,* or *u (catching, cold, cut)*.

Rule 20: The Final *k* Sound

The final *k* is usually spelled *-ck* in stressed syllables *(sick, thick)* and *-c* in unstressed syllables *(classic, traffic)*.

Exception

Tic—a muscle twitch (versus *tick*—the insect or the sound of a clock).

Rule 21: The *oi/oy* Sound

The *oi/oy* sound is usually spelled *oi* in the middle of a word *(joint)* and *oy* at the end *(toy)*.

Rule 22: The Letter *q*

The letter *q* is always followed by *u* in common English words.

Rule 23: The *-s* Suffix—Unusual Patterns

When *-s* is added to words to form the third-person, singular, present tense, *-es* must be added to verbs ending with "hissing" sounds (*ch, s, sh, x: catch, catches*). This is also true when adding *-s* to nouns. (See rule 7.)

Rule 24: *-sion* versus *-tion*

The *-sion* syllable is usually used where the pronunciation is *zhun* (voiced), as in *explosion,* or *shun* (not voiced), when the syllable is preceded by *l* or *s,* as in *passion* and *repulsion.* Other *shun* pronunciations are spelled *-tion (motion, traction)*.

The goal of teaching rules is not so much that writers will repeat them and puzzle over applying them for long periods as they write, but rather that the rules will become so programmed in their minds that they need no longer consciously think about them as they spell. The spelling will become a reflex, like brushing one's teeth, riding a bicycle, or driving a car.

Problem Areas in English Spelling

Lessons on problem areas in English spelling can also help students: these lessons will raise their awareness of spelling "pitfalls" and suggest approaches to avoid them. Problem areas that include a wide number of words and would be appropriate to teach to most classes will be labeled "C" for "class." Those more suited for individuals will be labeled "I" for "individual."

Problem Area 1: Compound, Segmented, Hyphenated Words (C)

Many words in English are often used together as pairs. These words may be written in one of three ways. Some remain separated, some are hyphenated, and some should be put together as one word (a compound word). Few fixed rules exist that tell us which way to combine these word pairs. Often, indeed, dictionaries will disagree. The reason is that the spellings represent a historical process. At first, the word pairs used together remain separated, retaining their individual identities *(school board, word processor, case study)*. Then some become linked through the use of a hyphen (self-expression). Finally, when they are so commonly used that they indeed almost form a new identity as a word, they merge completely, losing their hyphens *(roommate, classroom, typewriter)*. Some educational publications now use the word *casestudy*.

Students sometimes wish to hurry up the historical process and merge words that are not yet officially merged. The only solution is for them to memorize the commonly used pairs that they tend to link erroneously. Three of the most common word pairs that students wrongly merge are *high school, all right, (alright),* and *a lot*.

When students do combine words that should be combined, they sometimes misspell those words. For example, when the final letter of the first word is the same as the initial letter of the second, as in *roommate* or *overrate*, they tend to drop one letter *(roomate, overate)*. Here there is a spelling pattern that usually applies: simply put the two words together, retaining all letters.

Words that are midway into this historical process are often hyphenated, and in this transitional stage there can be inconsistency. Some dictionaries may spell a word-pair the traditional separate way, while others will link the same pair with a hyphen. The best thing to do is check a dictionary, and if it is not listed, to rely on one's own best judgment, as we did with *word-pair.* If the situation is indeed ambiguous, an individual's choice should not be considered an error. (For hyphens with compound adjectives and prefixes, see rule 9.)

Problem Area 2: Pronunciation and Spelling Mismatches (I or C)

When the spelling of a word does not match its standard pronunciation, errors often result (and English spelling is often non-acrophonic, as we pointed out in chapter 1). Many words have unpronounced letters or syllables in their spelling: *condemN, diffErent, IntErest, suRprise, usUally, dumB, deBt.* In all these cases, misspellings may result.

If a word's spelling does not correspond with its pronunciation, students should try to recognize the appearance of the word when it is correctly spelled, seeing that *crumb* without a *b* at the end *(crum)* or *sophomore* without a second *o (sophmore)* doesn't look right. However, if writers are mainly auditory spellers, they can memorize a separate "writing" pronunciation for the word—for example, hearing in their minds the *b* at the end of the word *crumb* when they write it, or pronouncing the second o in *sophomore.* (See "Exaggerated Pronunciations," p. 67.) A second technique is to associate the problem word with a related word that is pronounced more closely to the spelling: *muscle,* with its silent *c,* could be associated with *muscular,* in which the *c* is pronounced. (See Mnemonic Devices, "To Remember Words When Pronunciation Does Not Match Spelling," p. 62.)

Similarly, even when spelling and standard pronunciation correspond, variations in an individual's way of speaking can make spelling errors more likely. For example, some individuals may slur over sounds in particular words, saying *canidate* for *canDidate, enviroment* for *enviroNment, probley* for *proBAbly.* Or they may ADD a syllable that should not be there: *athElete* for *athlete.* Or they may mispronounce a sound slightly: *eXcape* for *eScape: eXspecially* for *eSpecially.*

On a broader scale, certain errors may be more common among speakers of a given dialect. Some regions of the country do not sound the first *h* in *which;* as a result, auditory spellers in that area may spell that word *wich.* Some dialects do not clearly pronounce particular consonants, so that we may get *futhermore* for *furthermore.* And some dialects make diphthongs of vowels—so that we get *steal* for *still*—or do not voice sounds in particular environments, so that we get *displace* for *displays*. The variations are numerous; volumes have been written on American dialects and regional English.

For our purposes, of course, teachers and writers need to recognize which words are misspelled because of such dialectal or individual variations in pronunciation. To correct the problem, writers might change their way of saying a word or simply memorize the spelling of words whose spelling does not correspond with the pronunciation in their dialect. Moreover, they need to develop their sensitivity to the appearance of words.

Problem Area 3: Unstressed Vowels (C)

Another pronunciation problem in English involves unstressed vowels—the schwa sound (ə), a soft "uh," like the final *a* in *sofa*. This sound can be represented by any of the English vowels (*a, e, i, o, u*) and even *y*. Thus we have *tolerANT, dEvelop, flexIble, authOr, murmUr,* and *synonYmous*. There is no way for a writer to determine which vowel represents the sound in any given word strictly on the basis of sound.

Thus, when a vowel's sound is not individualized, spelling problems often occur: is it *independence* or *independance*? *Grammer* or *grammar*? *Auther* or *author*? Strategies to avoid such errors are similar to those listed earlier in "Pronunciation and Spelling Mismatches." Students should try to recognize the appearance of the word when it is correctly spelled and realize that such misspellings as *author* spelled with an *e (auther)* look strange. They can memorize a separate "writing pronunciation" (authOR) or link the problem word with a related word that is pronounced more closely to the spelling (authORial). They can memorize mnemonic devices for particular problem words (see pp. 61–63). And they can check the spelling of unfamiliar words with unstressed vowels in the dictionary. If they are using a technical aid, such as an electronic speller or spell checker, and the aid indicates their version of the word is incorrect, but cannot offer the needed spelling, they can experiment with different vowels for the unstressed vowel until the computer can correct the word or indicates that they no longer have an error.

Problem Area 4: Sound-alike Letters (I)

Some students confuse letters or letter combinations that sound alike—or much alike—such as *s* and *c (sertain* for *certain)* or *d* and *t (modivation* for *motivation)*. Once the teacher and/or student recognize the confused pairs of letters or letter combinations, the student can be taught to look for these patterns and to check his or her spelling when the word contains those sounds. In addition, the student can memorize frequently used words that contain these sounds.

Problem Area 5: Homonyms (C)

Homonyms—words that sound alike but have different spellings and meanings—are also called *homophones, sound-alikes,* or *confusables*. According to Lunsford and Connors (1989, 353), these words cause the greatest number of spelling errors for college students, and according to Thomas Pollack (1971, 51) they are the third largest group of spelling errors for high school students. Since there is no particular rule for spelling these words, we as spelling teachers must raise student awareness of homonyms and near-homonyms, and students must memorize particular pairs that they as individuals tend to confuse.

Here are some pairs or trios of homonyms (alphabetized) that are the most frequently confused:

accept/except
affect/effect
its/it's
lead/led
principal/principle
their/there/they're
threw/through
to/too/two (usually the first two are confused)
weather/whether
whose/who's
your/you're

Another confusing type of homonym involves words that have merged and a corresponding pair that have kept their separate identities:

all ready/already
altogether/all together
every day/everyday

If students realize that a word is a homonym but do not remember the proper spelling for the meaning they want, they can check the form of the word they have spelled in a dictionary. There are also special dictionaries that list homonyms. Being aware of homonyms is important for students who use technical aids, for spell checkers on electronic typewriters and word processors will not catch homonym errors. Some electronic spellers do now designate common homonyms as such. (See also "To Remember Homonyms," which follows.)

Mnemonic Devices

A mnemonic (ni-món-ik) device (named for the Greek goddess of memory, Mnemosyne) is a technique used to help one remember something. It may be an association trick or acronym, a silly statement or an image—it can be anything, in fact, that *works*. (Often, the more ridiculous the device, the more likely it is to be remembered.) These devices work well for most students, particularly the learning disabled. Some mnemonics have already been given in conjunction with particular spelling rules and problems. Below is a collection of mnemonic devices which teachers may elect to offer to classes or individuals. Perhaps the best mnemonics, however, are those which the individual invents for his or her own personal misspellings. This collection can, indeed, serve as a model for such inventions.

To Remember Specific Segmented Words

All right is spelled like *all wrong*.
High school is spelled like *grade school*.
A lot is like *a little*.

To Remember Homonyms

The following devices help students remember the spelling of some specific homonyms:

> ACCEPT, EXCEPT: To *Accept* means to tAke; *EXcept* means EXclude.
>
> AFFECT, EFFECT: *Affect* is usually Action (a verb).
>
> EMIGRANT, IMMIGRANT: An Emigrant lEaves; an Immigrant comes In.
>
> HEAR, HERE: People HEAR with an EAR, and go from HERE to THERE.
>
> PRINCIPAL: The PRINCIPAL of your school is your PAL. PrincipAL is also your invested capitAL.
>
> STATIONARY, STATIONERY: *StationARY* means stAnding still; *stationERy* is writing papER.
>
> THEIR, THERE: *Their* refers to possession, and you give possessions to your HEIRS. *There* has *here* in it (both are directions).
>
> WEATHER, WHETHER: The wEAther is clEAr. *WHether* is like WHat.

To Remember Words When Pronunciation Does Not Match Spelling

When dealing with words that have a silent consonant, associate each word with a related word in a different form in which the problem letter is pronounced:

> muscle—musCular
>
> sign—siGnature

To Remember the Spelling of Words with Unstressed Vowels

CEMETERY: People get to a cEmEtEry with E's (ease).

CORRESPONDENCE: If you have to correspond by mail, you must be separated—and therefore cannot dance. (So it's -*dence,* not -*dance.*)

EXISTENCE: See INDEPENDENCE.

EXCELLENT: See INDEPENDENCE.

DEFINITE: There are a FINITE number of ways to spell *defInIte.*

GRAMMAR: Good grammAR gets you an *A.*

INDEPENDENCE: IndepenDENCE is an excellENT form of existENCE. (All end in -*ence* or -*ent.*)

PROFESSOR: To remember that *professOR* is spelled with a final *or,* think of "To profess OR not to profess."

RESISTANCE: On a picnic, one must often "resist ants."

SEPARATE: *SepArAte* rates two *A's;* there's a RAT in *sepARATe.*

TRANSPARENT: *Transparent* has *parent* in it; parents often see through their children.

Or associate the problem word with a related word in a different form in which the unstressed vowel becomes clear:

> author—authOrial
> definite—defInItive
> grammar—grammAtical
> labor—labOrious
> opposite—oppOse
> politics—polItical
> professOR—professOrial
> relative—relAte
> tolerant—tolerAte

To Remember Miscellaneous Spelling "Demons"

ACCOMMODATE: The word *accommodate* can accommodate two *c*'s, two *m*'s, and two *o*'s.

ARGUMENT: By the time the argument had ended, E had left.

COPYRIGHT: *Copyright* means the RIGHT to copy.

DESSERT: I always want seconds of deSSert (so two *s*'s).

ENVIRONMENT: There is IRON in our envIRONment.

GOVERNMENT: GoverNment goverNs.

OCCASION: Don't make an ASS of yourself when you spell *occasion* (double *c*, not double *s*).

SHEPHERD: A shepherd HERDS sheep.

SUCCESS: A cheer: S-U-C-C-E-S-S: That's the way you spell *success.*

VILLAIN: The VILLAIN is in his VILLA.

Activities and Techniques That Strengthen Visual and Auditory Skills

Besides lessons on rules and problem areas in English spelling, a number of specific activities and teaching techniques can be employed with classes or with individual students to strengthen the two major spelling routes—the visual and the auditory. Auditory activities will, of course, be most helpful for students who make little use of the sound of words and whose errors thus tend to be visual. Visual activities will be most helpful for students who make little use of the visual sense and so make mainly auditory errors. Some students may be weak in both routes and so will benefit from both kinds of activities. We have labeled each activity with the route or routes it is designed to strengthen.

Computer Games (Visual Route)

A number of recently developed computer spelling games, with their video-game-like qualities, can give individual students practice with increasing their visual memory and acuity—and provide a good time as well. These computer spelling games have available preprogrammed word lists suitable for advanced-level (high school or college) students. However, teachers can create, add to, or edit these word lists so that errors common to a particular group—or individual—can be included.

Most games are for two players; students might be paired for computer work in a writing center/lab or a classroom. However, as with most video games, spelling games designed for two can be played by one. Usually, students will have a list of the words that the computer is using for each game. Most games are provided with optional sound effects. Available games include the following:

1. *Dictionary.* The computer randomly selects a misspelled word from the assigned file and displays it on the screen. Players must correctly spell the misspelled word. (We suggest that the file include some correctly spelled words which the students must label as correct.)

2. *Hangman.* The computer selects a word from the assigned list, and then displays a gallows, below which is one dash for each letter in the word. The player guesses individual letters of the word. Each time the player guesses a wrong letter, another part of the body is displayed until the player is "hanged" or until the player guesses the last letter or the entire word. This is one of the most popular spelling games.

3. *Scrambled Eggs.* A word is selected from the spelling list and presented on-screen with the letters scrambled. The player who unscrambles the word receives a point for each letter in the word; if a player cannot unscramble the word, his or her opponent gets to try for bonus points.

4. *Spelling Bee.* A word is selected from the assigned list and displayed on the screen for two to three seconds. When the word disappears, the player must type in the word correctly; one point is awarded for each correct letter, and one subtracted for each mistake. This game is particularly good for developing a student's sense of the image of the whole word.

5. *Superguess.* The player is given a letter and asked to give a word from the selected spelling list containing that letter. If the player cannot think of a word containing that letter, he or she may request a different letter. After three such requests, the player loses his or her turn.

6. *Tic-Tac-Toe.* The computer displays the familiar 3 x 3 grid; players select a numbered square and can place an X or O in it by correctly filling in the missing letters of a word.

7. *Wordsearch.* The computer prints a grid made up of words from the list (horizontal or vertical) and then fills in the unoccupied spaces with random letters. The players must find the words in the grid and type them in. (These games are all available on Queue's "Lucky 7 Spelling Games" disk. For information write Queue, 338 Commerce Drive, Fairfield, CT 06430.)

Latent Study (Visual Route)

Edward Tolman describes a process of information acquisition that takes place just below the level at which it can be observed or demonstrated;

the learner is not aware that he or she is learning. This process accounts for the sudden flash of insight that sometimes seems to occur from nowhere.

In terms of spelling study, latent learning can be utilized by keeping the correctly spelled problem words in the speller's line of vision for a week—on the desk, on bookmarks, on the mirror in the bathroom. The words need not be directly studied. In a week, the correct spelling will often have been internalized by the student (Cates, 1982).

Correcting Misspelled Words (Visual Route)

There are a number of methods of correcting misspelled words that focus the student's visual attention on the parts of the word that are misspelled and generally heighten the visual sense of the correctly spelled word. We have already described Norman Hall's Letter Mark-Out System, in which students mark out any letter or letters missed in a word, write the correct letter or letters above the marked-out ones, and then rewrite the complete word to the side of the original misspelling (1962, 477).

A method using a similar principle has been suggested by Virginia Irwin (1971): she recommends that the teacher go over spelling lists and tests using an overhead projector, with color-coded transparencies that locate the problem letters in a word. Teachers can adapt this method to blackboards or handouts, underlining or capitalizing the common problem spots of a word. Examples:

bellIEf (rule 1)

comparAtive (problem area 2)

envIRONment (problem area 2)

Another suggestion is to have students write problem words using a different medium for the difficult spots—changing from ballpoint pen, for example, to crayon. This technique can heighten the motor, as well as visual, awareness of a word.

Focused and Realistic Proofreading (Visual Route)

In *focused* proofreading, students are given a passage with underlined spelling words they are to focus on and correct or label as correct. Example:

The girl <u>recieved</u> a letter in the mail and a package by <u>freight.</u>

In *realistic* proofreading, the passage resembles a real essay in that it must be proofread with no particular parts underlined. The student must check every word:

The girl recieved a letter in the mail and a package by freight.

(See also "Spelling Tests," pp. 73–75.)

Multiple Choice (Visual Route)

In multiple-choice spelling exercises, the student is given a choice of two or more spellings of a word; only one version is correct. The student must circle the correct spelling. Such exercises give the student practice in recognizing the correct spelling. Example:

The girl (received, recieved, reseeved) a letter.

(See "Spelling Tests," p. 74.)

Spelling Nonsense Words (Auditory Route)

To heighten the students' awareness of the relationship between spelling and sound, the teacher can dictate nonsense words, such as *lamash, glothe, smurgling,* and have the students guess a spelling. While sounds often do not accurately correlate with spelling in English, many of our locutions do have predictable spelling patterns—or choices of patterns. (See Hanna, 1963, described on pp. 45–47.) Thus discussions and comparisons of the "guessed" spellings can show students that certain sounds are often represented by one or two consistent spelling patterns (*-shun* = *-tion* or *-sion, -shul* = *-tial,* for example) and that some letters have different sounds (*c* can be pronounced hard [*k*] or soft [*s*]). Through this technique students can learn possible alternate spellings for their misspellings.

Syllabication (Auditory Route)

Students whose visual errors result in the omission of syllables might benefit from some exercises in dividing words into syllables. Hanna, Hodges, and Hanna (1971, 227–29) describe such exercises. In general, these exercises involve the teacher's explaining that each syllable must contain a vowel sound and possibly a number of consonant sounds as well. Then students are asked to divide nonsense words or some common English words into syllables and to pronounce them. Example:

supercalifragilisticexpialidocious =
    su per cal i frag i lis tic ex pi al i do cious

action = ac tion

literature = lit er a ture

Although a word may not be pronounced as its spelling would lead one to expect, there is usually enough correspondence that these exercises should help overly visual students recognize when important letters have been omitted.

Exaggerated Pronunciations (Auditory Route)

Another way to encourage the use of the auditory sense in spelling is to employ exaggerated pronunciations, whereby teacher and student emphasize the problem portion of the word when saying it. For example, the person who habitually leaves off the final *d* of *used* should practice pronouncing the word as "you said." Thus the student will encode the problem word auditorially as well as orthographically, thereby increasing the likelihood of remembering the correct spelling.

Oral Reading (Auditory Route)

Not only exaggerated pronunciation, but also "normal" pronunciation in oral reading can improve the auditory sense in spelling. Thus students might tape-record words from their individual spelling lists, use them in sentences, spell them, and then listen to these tapes.

Delayed Copying (Visual and Auditory Routes)

As explained by L. A. Hill (1969), delayed copying goes beyond simply automatically copying spelling words. Instead, this process combines several senses by asking the students to SEE, SAY, HEAR, and FEEL the word. First, they look at the whole word (SEE), then look away and pronounce it (SAY AND HEAR), and then they write it from memory, being aware of the physical process (FEEL). Only then do they check the word against the original. The process is repeated as necessary. One might also tell students to imagine words as if they were on a movie or television screen and to hold the image there as long as possible (Radaker, 1963).

Dictation (Visual and Auditory Routes)

The teacher dictates passages to students and has the students write them. The passages can include problem spelling words or words illustrating the current rule or lessons being studied. This exercise increases awareness of the relation between the auditory and the visual. (See "Spelling Tests," p. 73.)

Spelling Pairs (Visual and Auditory Routes)

Students are put into pairs with their individual spelling lists. They then drill each other from their partner's list. This exercise helps both the student playing the teacher and the student being drilled, as they see a word and say it, then hear it spelled (Buck, 1977).

Using the Dictionary

Specific training in spelling skills improves spelling, but spelling also improves when addressed in the general context of language study. Thus a unit on dictionary use develops spelling skills not only by virtue of practice in the basic process of locating words, but also by building an awareness of roots, parts of speech, and the history of language (the semantic route). Students will learn that the spelling itself, which appears as the first piece of information for a word's entry (with acceptable secondary spellings placed next) is only one of several pieces of information relevant to those seeking help with spelling. Other information is relevant as well:

1. *Word division,* indicated by dots or bars, separates a word into syllables, thereby indicating where a word can be divided at the end of a line.

2. *Pronunciation,* indicated in parentheses, is important because in many cases, words are easier to spell when they are pronounced in the standard way. The preferred pronunciation is given first, followed by alternates.

3. *Grammatical labels* will help the student recognize those homonyms that are different parts of speech (e.g., *advice* [n.] and *advise* [v.]).

4. *Grammatical forms* of a word given in the dictionary reveal how spelling may change when nouns become plurals, when adjectives are put into the comparative, superlative, or adverb form, or when different principal parts of a verb are used.

5. *Etymology,* the history of a word's evolution, often provides clues as to why a word is spelled as it is. (*The Oxford English Dictionary* is a rich resource for finding etymologies; the 1989 edition combines the original thirteen volumes and four supplements.)

6. *Definitions,* listed next, may be the only way to know if the writer has located the spelling of the desired word.

Teachers can give a number of interesting assignments that will teach students the potential of the dictionary:

1. They can ask students to break words down into their com-

ponent parts and define the individual meanings. (Most dictionaries list prefixes and suffixes.) Some words for investigation include *inborn, outgrow, unbreakable, forehead, nonsense, heaviness.* (See also "Word Elements," below.)

2. They can ask students to find the conjugated forms of regular and irregular verbs such as *dive, shave, drive.*

3. They can ask students to find the comparative, superlative, and adverb form of regular and irregular adjectives, such as *pretty* and *beautiful.*

4. They can have students look up the etymology of words such as *euphemism* and *narcissistic.*

Teachers can also recommend special spelling dictionaries. Alphabetical lists of words, unaccompanied by the information found in traditional dictionaries, can expedite the basic process of finding correct spelling. (And they are lighter to carry.) There are also dictionaries that list words as they are often misspelled, so that weak spellers can more easily find the words they are looking for. Webster's *New World Misspeller's Dictionary,* for example, first lists common misspellings and then gives their correct version. Sample entries:

compareable . . . *com pa ra ble*

comparitively . . . *com par a tive ly*

Other dictionaries emphasize phonetic misspellings and homonyms. A unique and particularly useful dictionary is Marvin L. Morrison's *Word Finder* (1987), which lists words according to their consonant sounds only. Thus *phone* is found under FN, while FNL locates *fennel, final, finale, finely, finial,* and *funnel.* Writers who rely heavily on the auditory route are often able to find the words they want in this dictionary. (Technical aids such as electronic spellers are discussed in "Computerized Spelling Aids," pp. 77–82.)

Word Elements

Poor spellers often lack a sense of the parts of words. They tend, indeed, to "think of words . . . only as arbitrary groupings of letters" (Grubgeld, 1986, 60).

Consider, for example, the frustration of a basic writer we observed as he tried to determine the spelling of *annuities.* He looked the word up under *e* and *i* and finally under *a,* but even then could not find it, for he thought the word had only one *n.* Had he known that its root was from the Latin *annus* (year)—the term means "a sum of money payable *yearly* or at regular intervals"—or had he simply related the word to *annual,* he could have more easily guessed the spelling. Consider, too, the numbers of basic writers who do not recognize common suffixes and prefixes—who spell the *dis-* prefix with two *s*'s or the *-ful* suffix with two *l*'s. No wonder so many basic writers often give up on trying to use a dictionary, asking helplessly, "How can I look it up if I can't spell it?"

Teaching word roots or semantic cores, prefixes, and suffixes can help develop students' sense of language, their semantic route: They will more clearly see that words are "like pieces of clay [which] . . . can be combined with other words to form larger pieces or . . . manipulated into a variety of shapes, depending upon their use in the sentence" (Shefter, 1976, 48). As words seem less arbitrary, students can guess more intelligently at how they are spelled. A unit on the dictionary can often be effectively combined with a study of the component parts of words. A number of texts present such material—for example, Elliot Smith's *Contemporary Vocabulary* (3rd ed., 1991). Below we give just a sampling of the kind of material that can be covered. Teachers will want to teach parts of words the students often use.

Prefixes

Teachers can present students with lists of common English prefixes (usually from Latin) and their meanings:

Prefix	Meaning	Example(s)
a-, ab-	away from	amoral, absent
ad-	to	adhere, admit
ante-	before	antebellum, antecedent
bi-	two	bisect, bicycle
circum-	around	circumstances
con-/com-	together	contact, convention
contra-	against	contradict, contrary
de-	from, down	descend, depress
dis-	apart, away	dissent, dismember
e-/ex-	out	extrovert, exclude
extra-	beyond	extracurricular extrasensory (perception)
in- (il-, im-, ir-)	in, into, on/not	immigrant, introvert irregular, illiterate
inter-	between	intercollegiate interrupt
intra-	among	intramurals
mis-	badly, wrongly	misspell, misuse

Prefix	Meaning	Example(s)
ob-	against, toward	obstacle
per-	through	performance, permeate
post-	after	postmortem, postpone
pre-	before	prescribe, premeditate
pro-	for	proclaim
re-	again	return, rehabilitate
semi-	part, half	semipro, semicircle
sub-	under	subterranean subordinate
super-	above	superintendent
trans-	across	transition, transfusion

By discussing word cores with different prefixes, teachers and students can illustrate the use of these prefixes, noting how words can be built and meaning and spelling ascertained. For instance, classes can discuss the differences in meaning in the words *amoral, immoral,* and *premoral.* Knowledge of prefixes can also clear up various points of student spelling confusion, such as that between *per* and *pre* words.

Teachers can further help students with spelling by explaining the process of assimilation, in which the last letter or sound of the prefix is absorbed or "assimilated" into the sound of the first letter of the word root. Usually this occurs to make pronunciation easier; for example, instead of "inmigrant," the word has become "immigrant": the *n* is assimilated into the *m* sound to make pronunciation easier. When such changes take place, the letter that stays is doubled:

ad + simulate = aSSimilate

ad + cept = aCCept

ex + centric = eCCentric

in + resistible = iRResistible

Most assimilative changes occur with seven prefixes—*ad-, com-, dis-, ex-, in-, ob-,* and *sub-.*

Word Roots

In illustrating word building with prefixes, it is only natural for teachers to present students with some basic Latin or Greek roots. The best to choose are those that form words the students often use and misspell; thus, again, those individual student spelling lists will be helpful. Some roots teachers might present include the following:

Latin or Greek Word	Meaning	English Word(s)
annus	year	annual, annuity
chron	time	chronological
cide	killing	suicide, homicide
finis	end, boundary	definite
frater	brother	fraternity
homo	alike, the same	homogenized
		homosexual
		homonym
log	word	monologue, logic
mis, mit	send, let	submit, submission
omni	all	omniscient
port	carry	portable
psyche	mind, soul	psychology, psyched
scio	know	science, conscience
soror	sister	sorority
the	God	atheism, theology

Suffixes

Finally, students can be shown how suffixes change parts of speech and add meaning. Some common suffixes include the following:

-ful (adj.—full of)	beautiful
-ible, able (adj., able to be—)	credible, legible
-ism (noun, belief in—)	atheism, Catholicism
-ist (noun, person who believes in—)	atheist, deist
-ize (verb, to make—)	legalize
-less (adj., without)	loveless, penniless
-ly (adv. from adj.)	quickly
-ment (noun from verb)	improvement
-ness (noun from adj.)	drunkenness
-ous (adj., full of)	credulous, curious
-tion (noun from verb)	creation, donation

Of course, students may invent words such as *moralless* or *unmoral* to mean without morals, when the existing word is *immoral;* but if they check their invented words in the dictionary or with a computerized spelling aid, they can eliminate such errors.

And certainly the positive side to the study of the component parts of words far outweighs any possible negative effect. Such a study not only enables students to recognize word meanings, but also helps them to make well-informed guesses as to how a word is spelled—the kind of guess that will yield better results from the dictionary or spelling aid.

Spelling Tests

Pretests

Arthur Gates (1931) and others have found that testing *before* studying spelling is an effective way of helping students find their areas of weakness. Moreover, if students find that they are weak spellers, they will, in most cases, be more interested in the spelling lesson to follow. Ann Dobie suggests opening each spelling session with a traditional spelling test of words illustrating the lesson of the week or day. (Dobie, 1986, suggests twenty words, though the number can vary.) Teachers read the list of words to the students, using each word in a simple sentence. Because students are more interested in learning to spell words that really are in their writing vocabularies, some (if possible, all) of the words should be drawn from papers written by the class. If a teacher's class has not yet written that many papers, teachers may find a "bank" of spelling errors from former students handy to use. (See "Forming a Spelling Error Bank," p. 45.)

After the pretest, the particular rule or lesson regarding the words is given. Many of the words given on the pretest could be used as illustrations; then a self-check of the pretest can follow, often using some of the visual techniques described earlier.

Posttests

A test to show how well the students can apply each lesson covered in class should follow soon after. Posttests may be simply repeats of the pretest, but they can do more for the students if they allow the students to exercise different spelling routes as they apply the lesson. For the "spelling" composition class, McAlexander, Gregg, and Winger developed tests that include five basic components. Auditory skills are tested in part I of the test, a dictation: the teacher reads aloud five sentences which students are to write out in full. Each sentence contains at least one spelling word relating to the week's lesson or rule. The following sentence, for example, gives points for two spelling words from the lesson on homonyms: *witch-which* and *too-to*:

My typewriter, *which* I've used for ten years, is *too* old-fashioned.

As teachers grade these sentences, they can note other errors (even if points are not subtracted for them) and include instruction on those errors in future classes. The above sentence, for example, served to reveal problems with compound and hyphenated words *(typewriter, old-fashioned)*.

While part I stresses auditory skills, parts II, III, and IV, which are given in traditional written form, test visual skills in order of increasing difficulty. The dictated part of the test is collected before these three parts are handed out, so that students cannot get answers to their dictation from the rest of the test. (Also, part I can be graded as students work on the other three parts.)

Part II is a multiple-choice section: students are given a number of sentences and, for each, asked to choose one of two spellings for the target word:

Tom wanted (apart, a part) of the action.

This section of the test requires students to develop their visual discrimination—the sense of a word's *looking* right—as they choose between two versions of a word. Such choices also give students with ineffective visual skills practice in employing other routes to help with the selection of the correct word—for example, applying a rule, sounding out a word, or simply memorizing a commonly used word.

Part III involves focused proofreading: students are given a paragraph with highlighted sections they are to focus on and either correct or label correct. Here, for example, is a paragraph testing the "*i* before *e*" rule:

The Wall Street businessman with the *briefcase* had a smug, *conceited* look on his face. He apparently felt that he had *acheived* the pinnacle of success. He did not see the *theif* sneaking up behind him. When he felt a quick tug on his arm, he thought a *freind* was trying to get his attention. Too late he realized that his *breifcase* had disappeared. The businessman let out a *shriek* of *greif;* he did not look *conceited* anymore.

Students were to label the first *briefcase* and *conceited* as correct, but change *acheived* to *achieved* and so on. Giving words more than once helps students become more aware of consistency in spelling.

Part IV is a paragraph of "realistic proofreading." This paragraph more closely resembles a real essay in that it must be proofread and corrected with no particular parts given visual emphasis. Thus the paragraph about the businessman would be given without any words underlined, and students would be told to correct any misspellings involving the "*i* before *e*" rule.

Teachers might also give a review proofreading paragraph that includes spelling words from lessons of previous weeks, or include review words in the realistic proofreading paragraph. To increase the students' interest in these quizzes, one of these proofreading paragraphs might be a part of a humorously melodramatic continued story; students have to wait with bated breath until next week's corresponding quiz paragraph to find out what happens.

Part V reinforces the students' memory of words that they as individuals have misspelled. As students hand in their tests, they show the teacher their individual spelling lists, in whatever form they have been assigned. The teacher selects from one to three of the words and dictates them to the student, who writes them down at the end of the test.

Such tests, given weekly, take from twenty minutes to a half hour of class time. They are returned during the next class and reviewed, a process that further reinforces the tested material. Teachers may choose to correct the tests themselves or to have the students correct their own. Recent research has suggested that the self-corrected test is effective as a learning technique, but that it should not be used exclusively (Allred, 1977, 24). Often it is best to have the students correct their own pretests, while teachers correct the posttests. Most important, of course, is to keep students exercising their spelling skills so that they will be able to apply those skills in their future writing.

Proofreading Techniques

As we stated earlier, spelling instruction is most effective when it is embedded in a meaning-centered, process-oriented pedagogy. The lessons, activities, and tests described above should be integrated into a curriculum involving reading, discussion, and writing about ideas and experiences. The ultimate indicator of spelling success is not how high the grades on the spelling tests are but how well the students apply spelling techniques to their own writing. Thus, in addition to spelling instruction, students need to be taught proofreading techniques.

To begin, of course, students need to understand the part that proofreading (checking carefully and purposefully for "surface" errors— i.e., grammatical and mechanical errors) and editing (correcting those errors) play in the writing process. Teachers should stress the fact that it is best to separate those tasks from the other stages of writing— prewriting, when ideas are born and experimented with; drafting, when a preliminary version of the text is created; and revising, which entails seeing the entire script with a critical eye toward making full-scale changes in content and organization in a further draft or drafts. During these stages, students might notice and correct errors, but errors should not be the main concern. Only when these other tasks have been completed should the writer check the manuscript with the *main* purpose of seeing that it is error-free. Even though some students may consider the proofreading and editing stage of writing tedious, teachers need to stress the importance of knowing that one's manuscript is the best it can be—with no errors distracting the reader from its content. And checking for misspellings is, of course, one of the major tasks of proofreading.

With handwritten texts, the job of proofreading for spelling errors is more difficult—and more important as well—since handwritten papers tend to contain more mechanical errors than do typed papers. The writer must catch slips of the pen and illegible handwriting, proceeding on the assumption that every illegible letter or word might be interpreted as a misspelling. Regardless of whether a manuscript is typed or handwritten, however, there are a number of specific methods for catching misspelled words. Students with spelling weaknesses might be advised to employ one or more of the following techniques:

1. Place a ruler or a large card under each line to focus concentration and vision.

2. Cut an average word-length block out of an index card and move it along the lines, word by word, to check for misspellings (Anderson, 1987). This technique will focus the proofer's attention on the individual word and help keep him or her from being distracted by the material itself. Homonyms, however, will need to be judged in context.

3. Read the manuscript backwards, from the last sentence to the first. Again, however, students should be warned to check homonyms in context.

4. Read the paper aloud, looking carefully at each word as it is pronounced.

5. Choose a proofreading partner, and have one person read aloud as the other looks at the manuscript.

Other advice teachers can give students includes the following:

1. Remind students to read their papers (whether aloud or silently) slowly. Rapid reading makes it difficult to focus on each word and letter.

2. Remind students to look particularly for words they have misspelled before (familiarity with their individual spelling lists is helpful here) and to be aware of homonyms.

When possible, teachers might have the students put the papers aside for a day or two (or return student papers uncorrected a day or two after they have been handed in); then they can direct students to proofread the papers again. Fresh eyes are less likely to supply missing letters or put reversed ones in proper sequence.

Computerized Spelling Aids

Finally, of course, there is technology to help the weak speller. Teachers can introduce their students to three computerized spelling aids: type-writers with spell checkers, electronic spellers, and word-processing programs with spell checkers. All of them have built-in dictionaries against which the spell checker's computer checks words. They all involve some expense and require some skills to use effectively, and they are not without their drawbacks; but these devices can be a great help to many weak spellers.

Typewriters with Spell Checkers

Most of these typewriters have off/on buttons for their spell checkers. When the checker is on, a bell (like that used when the margin has been violated) alerts typists to questionable words (i.e., words not in the typewriter's dictionary). Of course, the bell also rings for typographical errors, proper names, technical terms, and any other word not found in its dictionary, though often words can be *added* to the dictionary to avoid some unnecessary rings. Because these spell checkers may break the concentration of writers who compose on the typewriter, some individuals write out first drafts of their essay by pen, or type them with the spell checker off, and then type the final draft using the spell checker.

Electronic Spellers

A number of the small, hand-held, battery-run, electronic spellers have come on the market in the past few years. Physically, they resemble a calculator, but instead of numbers, they have a miniature typewriter (or alphabetical) keyboard. To check a spelling, the student types in a version of a word. If the speller's computer cannot find that version of the word in its usually 80,000-or-more-word dictionary, the display offers, in a matter of seconds, one or more suggestions that are visually or phonetically close to the typed-in word. If the student types in "occurance," for example, the display will show "occurrence"; if the student types in "enhanse," most spellers will show "enhance"—and then several other possibilities in order of closeness, from "inhale" to "immense."

If the word is found in the speller's dictionary, the speller will indicate that the word is correct. If the student suspects the "correct" word to be an incorrect homonym, he or she can still call up a list of similar words, thus getting, for example, *principle* for *principal*. Recently appearing on the market is a model that can help the student choose the correct homonym by indicating "confusables" (its term) with a question mark. This speller will, upon request, give brief (usually one-word) definitions of these confusables. For example, *bare* will be preceded by a *?*; the definition is *naked,* and one alternate is given: *bear,* defined as *carry.* Higher-priced spellers include a thesaurus or dictionary with a larger display; these give fuller, more complete definitions of most typed-in words (not just confusables).

Because they are relatively inexpensive and so easily portable (unlike a typewriter or word processor), these spellers are very useful. Writing labs, English departments, and school libraries may wish to purchase a few spellers to lend to individuals, but many students will no doubt wish to purchase one of their own. An electronic speller will be most effectively used by writers with an accurate sense of doubt about their spelling and the ability to recognize (if not produce) the correct word. Many students can learn to be efficient users of electronic spellers, thereby increasing their writing confidence and eliminating a large percentage of their spelling errors (McAlexander, 1988).

Spell Checkers in Word Processors

Perhaps the greatest technological breakthrough for spellers is the spell checker in word-processing programs. Most word-processing programs today have built-in spell checkers (as opposed to those that have to be used separately). When using a spell checker, the writer requests the computer to identify any word in the text that is not in its dictionary. The computer then highlights those words and, like the electronic speller, offers the writer the choice of a number of words that are visually or phonetically close to the misspelling. With many programs, the writer can request the computer to make the choice.

These spell checkers have been a particular boon to the learning disabled. Christopher Lee no doubt speaks for many LD students when he says, "I did not learn how to write until I learned how to use a computer. . . . In my past, writing was spelling, and since I could not spell, I could not write" (Lee and Jackson, 1992, 23). The improvement of poor spellers on the computer is not just because of the corrections provided, however; using a spell checker can stengthen the writer's auditory and visual spelling routes. The processor's producing a clear image of the words often helps students with visual-processing weaknesses (as well as those with poor handwriting) to see the word more clearly. Moreover, repeatedly missing a word and having to choose the correct version from the screen helps reinforce the correct image of the word in students' minds. Auditory skills can be developed if students are encouraged to play with misspellings so far off from the target word that the computer can label them as misspelled but cannot correct them. Students can be advised to sound out words more carefully or to try different vowels for unstressed vowels (the schwa). One of our students, for example, wrote *sourety* for *sorority*. When the computer highlighted the word as misspelled but did not come up with the desired word in its list of suggestions, he tried sounding out the word, realized a sound was missing in his misspelling, and rewrote the word as *sororety*. This time the computer was able to identify the word he wanted. Had it not, the student could have actually found the correct spelling by using the second technique—substituting other vowels for the unstressed final vowel. With such auditory and visual practice through the use of the spell checker, a number of students report that they begin to spell more words correctly in the first place.

Computers offer other services as well. Sometimes a writer has repeatedly misspelled a word throughout the text. In such cases, many programs offer *search* and *search and replace* commands which can help the writer find and correct each instance of that particular misspelled word. The search command will locate every use of a word in a text, allowing the writer to make sure it is spelled correctly. The search and replace command not only locates a word, it also replaces every instance of it with the correct spelling.

Word-processing spell checkers, of course, have a vast advantage over the electronic spellers in that they will locate errors for the writer upon his or her request. They are also superior to typewriters with spell checkers, because the writer can request that the document's spelling be checked *after* the document is completed, thus avoiding the bell-ringing distraction.

Differing Abilities of Computerized Spelling Aids

Of course, some computerized spelling aids work better than others. The number of words in a program's dictionary can vary from 50,000 to 130,000; and spell checkers may be programmed differently. Thus some programs will find errors more accurately and, in the case of electronic spellers and word-processing spell checkers, come up with more and better choices for a misspelled word. While one program we checked (Professional Write) offered only such alternatives as *allspice* for a student's misspelling of *alcohol*, another (The Franklin Spelling Ace) was able to offer the desired word when given the same misspelling. A study described by Meyer, Pisha, and Rose (1991, 121–22) found that of 146 non-word spelling errors made by LD adolescents, Bank Street Writer, the most effective word-processing spell checker of the Apple II family programs tested, suggested the correct spelling for 63 percent, while MacWrite II, the most effective checker on the Macintosh, did so for 82 percent. Also, while search times will vary according to how far off the misspelling is, some computer programs simply work faster than others. It may take one program fifteen seconds, another twenty-five seconds, to offer options for the same misspelling.

Finally, in word processors, some spell-checking programs are easier to use than others. One program may let the writer check the spelling of the word or the paragraph on which the cursor is resting; others work only on the words on a single page and/or the words in the entire document. Another difference in word-processing programs may be significant for poor spellers. Students who are "right-brained" and thus picture-oriented rather than word-oriented (see "Logographic versus Alphabetic Systems," p. 1) might do better with word-processing programs that include an icon or logograph with their directions. For example, Macintosh's MacWrite includes a picture of a scroll and feather with its "create a document" option, a manila folder indicating that a file can be created, and an exploding bomb with its message, "A system error has occurred."

Current books and periodicals that describe and compare a number of word-processing programs can help one choose the best word-processing/spell-check program for a particular teacher, group of students, or school.

Limitations of Computerized Spelling Aids

For all that these computerized spelling aids can do, they are not foolproof. For one thing, they cannot detect all errors. Computers will not recognize homonym errors as misspellings, since these words are found in the program's dictionary. Similarly, if a student's misspelling of a target word is actually another word in the dictionary, that error will not be identified. For example, if a student spells *financial* as *finical*, the computer will not catch the error, since *finical* is a word which means *finicky*. Nor will spell checkers (the ones we tested, at any rate) point out as errors nonstandard spellings that are included in dictionaries (*alright*, for example).

Even when a spell checker detects an error, the computer cannot always offer the correct spelling. For instance, when *alcohol* was spelled *allchol,* and when *high school* and *a lot* were not segmented, the programs we tested could not come up with any of the three desired words. Moreover, the computer may give only two or three forms of the target word—for example, the adjective or noun form, but not the verb form that the student wants. And as we have already noted, a spell checker may be able to list the correct spellings for only about 60 to 80 percent of a dysgraphic student's errors.

Furthermore, if the desired word is in the list of options offered by the computer, and the writer asks the computer to make the selection (in programs offering that service), the computer's choice may not be correct. Those same two "most effective" programs in the study described by Meyer, Pisha, and Rose—Bank Street Writer and MacWrite II—listed the correct spelling first in the list of alternative spellings only 38 percent and 48 percent of the time (1991, 122). The capacities and limitations of a typical word-processing spell checker are illustrated in figures 23 and 24, which show a page of student text before and after he had used the spell checker. This program was able to correct seventeen of twenty-five errors, or 68 percent.

As computerized spelling aids are refined and improved, a number of their limitations are being eliminated. For instance, words—such as names and technical terms—can now be added to computer dictionaries in typewriters and word processors so that these words will not be identified as errors. Moreover, at least two software packages (WriteRight and The Sensible Grammar) identify homonyms. Both give the writer a choice of two methods of identification. One is for the computer to identify homonyms while the text is being created. However, this process can be distracting, like the typewriter's spell-checker bell. Or, when the text is complete, the computer will list all the homonyms the writer has used; then the writer must go back and find those homonyms. This process can be time-consuming, even if the writer uses the search command. Still, for students who miss many homonyms, these programs are helpful. Style-checking programs may also be of help. MLA's new Editor (1991), for instance, is programmed to find many nonstandard spellings, missing or unnecessary hyphens, improperly formed compounds, and some homonym errors. And, as we have said, at least one type of electronic speller now on the market does identify and briefly define homonyms.

Current research is attempting to determine if and how the use of computers helps basic writers throughout the writing process. While the results of these studies are mixed, one fact seems clear: in spite of

> I come from a very large family, and to me (haveing)[1] a large family has many (advantage)[2] (whan)[3] you have as many people in (youer)[4] family as I do (alot)[5] of relatives go into many (differant)[6] (profesions)[7] that can work to (youer) advantage. large (familys)[8] also help the house chores go by quicker and can give you more (independance)[9] and freedom.
>
> (Haveing)[10] (alot) of (relitives)[11] can be very profitable when it comes to illnesses or (needes.)[12] In my family I have an uncle that is a doctor.this comes in handy when I get (hart)[13] or need advice or medical (seplyes.)[14] For (examply)[15] a couple of weeks ago I (drop)[16] a large log on my ankle and thought I had broken something.So I went to my uncles office and got him to x-ray it for free.Every year me and my brother and sisters get a (tetnes)[17] shot because I live on a farm and get (alot) of cuts and scratches from rusty old nails or scrap metal.this is another time my uncle comes in handy because he can get these shots for us.also when my sisters wanted to get (there)[18] ears (pearst)[19] my uncle did it (to.)[20] it is very handy having a doctor in the family.
>
> Because of where I live I have many (responsibilitys)[21] put on me.there is (alwayes)[22] something to do,like (geting)[23] and keeping the house in supply of firewood,haying the (horseses,)[24] and building on the barn,a (shead,)[25] or adding onto our house.

Figure 23. Pre–spell-check page from student essay. The student has 25 misspellings (numbered and circled by the teacher). The count includes morphological errors (missing endings) and does not count repeated errors. Some errors may be motor (typographical) errors.

the differences among computer programs and in spite of a number of general limitations, computerized technical aids can greatly improve writers' spelling and thus their confidence in writing. Moreover, simply being aware of the limitations of these spelling aids can help writers use them more effectively.

I come from a very large family, and to me having a large family has many (advantage.) When you have as many people in your family as I do (alot) of relatives go into many different professions that can work to your advantage. Large families also help the house chores go by quicker and can give you more independence and freedom.

Having (alot) of relatives can be very profitable when it comes to illnesses or needs. In my family I have an uncle that is a doctor. This comes in handy when I get (hart) or need advice or medical (selfish.) For example a couple of weeks ago I (drop) a large log on my ankle and thought I had broken something. So I went to my uncles office and got him to x-ray it for free. Every year me and my brother and sisters get a tetanus shot because I live on a farm and get (alot) of cuts and scratches from rusty old nails or scrap metal. This is another time my uncle comes in handy because he can get these shots for us. Also when my sisters wanted to get (there) ears pierced my uncle did it (to.) it is very handy having a doctor in the family.

Because of where I live I have many responsibilities put on me. There is always something to do, like getting and keeping the house in supply of firewood, haying the horses, and building on the barn, a shed, or adding onto our house.

Figure 24. The same page, post–spell check. This spell checker was able to detect and correct 17 of the 25 errors, or 68 percent. The remaining errors are circled. There were six errors the computer did not detect: (1) *advantage* for *advantages;* (2) *alot* for *a lot* (the computer disk may have needed cleaning, since usually the checker found that error); (3) *hart* for *hurt;* (4) *drop* for *dropped;* (5) *there* for *their;* (6) *to* for *too.* The computer was able to detect but not correct two errors: (1) *seplys* for *supplies* (it suggested *selfish* and *sepias*) and (2) *pearst* for *pierced* (the instructor supplied the correct spelling, since the computer gave no suggestions). Had the spell check identified *alot* as an error (as this program usually does), it would have given as suggested spellings *alit, allot, Alta, alto,* and *aloft.*

Conclusion

So what happens when a high school or college teacher stops merely marking spelling errors with the "sp" label—or ignoring spelling errors—and begins a specific program designed to improve spelling? Do the students' errors disappear after ten or fifteen weeks, or after a school year's worth of such training in the usual English curriculum?

The answer, of course, is no. But the experience of many teachers has shown that the spelling of most students will improve—and that the spelling of particularly weak spellers may improve dramatically. Let us look at what happened to the poor spellers described in our Introduction after they received specific help (technological and/or pedagogical) for their problems.

Dick, the student in the developmental studies program who was making an average of one misspelling in every thirty-eight words, was given a program of individual help with spelling during his second quarter in the program. On the final exam he had reduced his errors to one per hundred words: *loosing (losing), Olypics (Olympics), your (you're), recieve (receive,* although he spelled that word correctly eight other times), *to (too)* and *than (then).* Not only does his essay have fewer errors, but those errors are also closer to the target words than the misspellings he had been making. (Indeed, the last three may have been motor errors.) Dick exited the developmental program, successfully completed his first-year English courses, and is now maintaining a *B* average at his university.

Tracy was the student evaluated at her university's Learning Disabilities Adult Clinic and diagnosed not as learning disabled, but as having a visual-processing weakness that caused her overreliance on the auditory route. For her third quarter in developmental studies, Tracy was placed in a spelling-focused composition class. She continued to have good content and organization; at the same time, the class training helped her to eliminate many of her most common spelling errors. She exited the developmental program at the end of that quarter and went on to successfully complete her freshman English courses. (More about Tracy is found in McAlexander and Gregg, 1989.)

Tom, the young man who was self-conscious every time he had to write a check, finally decided to audit one of the spelling composition classes offered in the university's developmental studies program before enrolling in regular freshman composition. In that class he was given a number of lessons in spelling and was introduced to an electronic spelling aid. By the end of the term his spelling errors were reduced significantly, and he felt confident about going on to his freshman English course—which he successfully completed.

In spite of the misgivings of some of his school's LD clinicians, Charles stayed on as a student at the university and began taking part in a learning disabilities tutorial program. With intensive tutoring, the help of his teachers, and much hard work, Charles was able not only to pass his freshman English courses, but also to produce creative, sensitive essays with very few errors. He began using a word processor, gave encouraging talks to other LD students, and graduated—as he had been determined to do.

Arthur, the student inexperienced with Standard English, whose spelling errors lowered his exam grade so severely, did exit the developmental writing program the following quarter. He enrolled in one of his university's first computer-assisted composition courses—and made an *A*.

Finally, there is Peter, the talented student who left college after getting a *D* in freshman composition. Several months later he decided to return to the university and be evaluated by its learning disabilities clinic. He was diagnosed as dysgraphic, with particular problems in spelling. Peter illustrates the possible hereditary factor with dysgraphia: years before, a close relative of his had had the same problem and never finished high school. Peter was luckier; now, as an LD student, he is able to use word processors for his writing (including essay tests). Not only is Peter doing well academically, but he is also appearing in a number of dramatic productions, revealing considerable talent as an actor.

As these students' stories suggest, in times past, too many able students fell by the wayside because poor spelling made them look—and feel— illiterate. They failed English courses; they dropped out of high school; they did not complete college. Now, with understanding and encouragement, training in spelling, and technology, many students with these problems pass and graduate—and many perform with distinction.

References

Allred, R. A. 1977. *Spelling: The Application of Research Findings.* Washington, D.C.: National Education Association.

Anderson, K. A. 1987. "Using a Spelling Survey to Develop Basic Writers' Linguistic Awareness: A Response to Ann B. Dobie." *Journal of Basic Writing* 6: 72–78.

Anthony, B. M. 1971. "Why Keep Spelling in the Curriculum?" *Education* 92: 130–33.

Benson, J. H., and A. G. Carey. 1940. *The Elements of Lettering.* Newport, R.I.: John Stevens.

Berlin, J. A. 1987. *Rhetoric and Reality: Writing Instruction in American Colleges, 1900–1985.* Carbondale: Southern Illinois University Press.

Brown, J. I., and T. E. Pearsall. 1985. *Better Spelling: Fourteen Steps to Spelling Improvement.* Lexington, Massachusetts: D. C. Heath.

Buck, J. L. 1977. "A New Look at Teaching Spelling." *College English* 38: 703–06.

Butler, J. F. 1987 [1981]. "Remedial Writers: The Teacher's Job as Corrector of Papers." In *A Sourcebook for Basic Writing Teachers,* edited by T. Enos, 557–64. New York: Random House.

Cates, W. M. 1982. "Do or Die Spelling: Teaching without the Struggle." *English Journal* 71(1): 45–47.

Conley, J. 1974. Speling. *College Composition and Communication* 25: 243–46.

Connors, J. 1980. "Will Spelling Count?" *Chronicle of Higher Education,* June 2, 48.

Connors, R. J., and A. A. Lunsford. 1988. "Frequency of Formal Errors in Current College Writing, or Ma and Pa Kettle Do Research." *College Composition and Communication* 39: 395–409.

Cromer, R. 1980. "Spontaneous Spelling by Language Disordered Children." In *Cognitive Processes in Spelling,* edited by U. Frith, 405–22. New York: Academic Press.

Cross, P. 1971. *Beyond the Open Door.* San Francisco: Jossey-Bass.

Davis, Z. 1987. "Upper Grades Spelling Instruction: What Difference Does It Make?" *English Journal* 76(3): 100–01.

Dobie, A. B. 1986. "Orthographical Theory and Practice, or How to Teach Spelling." *Journal of Basic Writing* 5: 41–48.

Foran, T. 1934. *The Psychology and Teaching of Spelling.* Washington, D.C.: Catholic Education Press.

Gates, A. I. 1931. "An Experimental Comparison of the Study-Test and Test-Study Method in Spelling." *Journal of Education* 22: 1–19.

Gregg, N., C. Hoy, and R. Sabol. 1988. "Spelling Error Patterns in Normal, LD, and Underprepared College Writers." *Journal of Educational Assessment* 6: 14–23.

Grubgeld, E. 1986. "Helping the Problem Speller without Suppressing the Writer." *English Journal* 75(2): 58–61.

Hahn, J. 1990. "How Do You Spell?" *Visions and Revisions: Research for Writing Teachers.* 3–13.

Hairston, M. 1981. "Not All Errors are Created Equal: Nonacademic Readers in the Professions Respond to Lapses in Language." *College English* 43: 794–806.

———. 1982. "The Winds of Change: Thomas Kuhn and the Revolution in the Teaching of Writing." *College Composition and Communication* 33: 76–88.

Hall, N. 1962. "Individualize Your Spelling Instruction." *Elementary English* 39: 476–77.

Hanna, P. R. 1963. "Phoneme-Grapheme Correspondences as Cues to Spelling Improvement." Stanford University School of Education. Report number CRP 1991, 1955. ERIC ED 003 321.

Hanna, P. R., R. E. Hodges, and J. S. Hanna. 1971. *Spelling: Structure and Strategies.* Boston: Houghton Mifflin.

Harris, G. W. 1966. *Sut Lovingood's Yarns.* Edited by M. T. Inge. New Haven, Connecticut: College and University Press.

HEATH (Higher Education and Adult Training for People with Handicaps) Resource Center. 1987. "Learning Disabled Adults in Postsecondary Education." One Dupont Circle, NW, Suite 670, Washington, D.C., 20036-1193.

Hill, L. A. 1969. "Delayed Copying." *English Language Teaching* 23: 238–39.

Hillocks, G., Jr. 1986. *Research on Written Composition: New Directions for Teaching.* Urbana, Illinois: ERIC Clearinghouse on Reading and Communication Skills and the National Conference on Research in English.

Hodges, J. C. 1941. *Harbrace Handbook of English.* New York: Harcourt, Brace and Company.

Hook, J. N. 1986. *English 1500.* San Diego: Harcourt Brace Jovanovich.

Hull, G., and M. Rose. 1989. "Rethinking Remediation: Towards a Social-Cognitive Understanding of Problematic Reading and Writing." *Written Communication* 6: 139–54.

Irving, J. 1983. "How to Spell." *Power of the Printed Word.* New York: International Paper Co., Dept. 12, P.O. Box 954, Madison Square Station, New York, N.Y. 10010.

Irwin, V. 1971. "Reds, Greens, Yellows Ease the Spelling Blues." *Missouri English Bulletin* 28: 1–8.

Jarvis, O. T. 1963. "How Much Time for Spelling?" *Instructor* 73: 59, 156.

Lazarus, B. D. 1989. "Serving Learning Disabled Students in Postsecondary Settings." *Journal of Developmental Education* 12: 2–6.

Leathers, L. M. III. 1990. Interview by P. J. McAlexander, July 15, Athens, Georgia.

Lee, C. M., and R. F. Jackson. 1992. *Faking It: A Look into the Mind of a Creative Learner.* Upper Montclair, N.J.: Boynton/Cook.

Lunsford, A., and R. J. Connors. 1989. *The St. Martin's Handbook.* New York: St. Martin's Press.

Lunsford, A., and P. A. Sullivan. 1990. "Who Are Basic Writers?" In *Research in Basic Writing: A Bibliographic Sourcebook,* edited by M. G. Moran and M. J. Jacobi, 17–30. New York: Greenwood Press.

McAlexander, P. J. 1988. "Electronic Spellers." *English Journal* 77(8): 65.

McAlexander, P., and N. Gregg. 1989. "The Roles of English Teachers and LD Specialists in Identifying Learning Disabled Writers: Two Case Studies." *Journal of Basic Writing* 8: 72–86.

McClellan, J. 1978. "A Clinic for Misspellers." *College English* 40: 324–29.

Meyer, A., B. Pisha, and D. Rose. 1991. "Process and Product in Writing: Computer as Enabler." In *Written Language Disorders: Theory into Practice,* edited by A. M. Bain, L. L. Bailet, and L. S. Moates, 99–128. Austin, Texas: Pro-Ed.

Morrison, M. L. 1987. *Word Finder: The Phonic Key to the Dictionary.* San Diego: Pilot Light.

Noguchi, R. R. 1991. *Grammar and the Teaching of English: Limits and Possibilities.* Urbana, Illinois: National Council of Teachers of English.

Pei, M. 1952. *The Story of English.* New York: J. B. Lippincott.

Pollack, T. C. 1971. "Misspelling in Grades 9–12." *English Record* 22: 44–53. ERIC ED 059 190.

Radaker, L. D. 1963. "The Effect of Visual Imagery upon Spelling Performance." *Journal of Educational Research* 56: 370–72.

Richards, A. 1985. "College Composition: Recognizing the Learning Disabled Writer." *Journal of Basic Writing* 4: 65–79.

Sharknas, J. 1970. "Individualized Spelling." *Instructor* 79: 64.

Shaughnessy, M. P. 1976. "Basic Writing." In *Teaching Composition: Ten Bibliographic Essays,* edited by Gary Tate, 137–68. Fort Worth: Texas Christian University Press.

———. 1977. *Errors and Expectations.* New York: Oxford University Press.

Shefter, H. 1976. *6 Minutes a Day to Perfect Spelling.* New York: Simon and Schuster.

Shen, G. 1990. Interview by P. J. McAlexander, December 13, University of Georgia, Athens.

Sloan, G. 1979. "The Subversive Effects of an Oral Culture on Student Writing." *College Composition and Communication* 30: 156–60.

Smith, C. R. 1991. *Learning Disabilities: The Interaction of Learner, Task, and Setting,* 2nd ed. Boston: Allyn and Bacon.

Smith, E. L. 1991. *Contemporary Vocabulary,* 3rd ed. New York: St. Martin's Press.

Stirling, E. 1989. "The Adolescent Dyslexic: Strategies for Spelling." *Annals of Dyslexia* 39: 268–78.

Troyka, L. Q. 1987. "Defining Basic Writing in Context." In *A Sourcebook for Basic Writing Teachers,* edited by T. Enos, 2–15. New York: Random House.

Venezky, R. L. 1967. "English Orthography: Its Graphical Structure and Its Relation to Sound." *Reading Research Quarterly* 2(3): 75–105.

Walsh, L. 1967. *Read Japanese Today.* Quoted in *Learning to Spell* by R. E. Hodges, 1981. Urbana, Illinois: National Council of Teachers of English.

Additional Recommended Readings

Barbe, W. B., A. S. Francis, and L. A. Braun, eds. 1982. *Spelling: Basic Skills for Effective Communication.* Columbus, Ohio: Zaner-Bloser.

Drake, W. D. 1967. *The Way to Spell: A Guide for the Hesitant Speller.* Scranton, Pennsylvania: Chandler Publishing Company.

Hodgins, M. G. 1968. *You Can Spell.* Toronto: McGraw-Hill.

Kitzhaber, A. R. 1953. "Rhetoric in American Colleges, 1850–1900." Diss. University of Washington.

McCrumb, R., W. Cran, and R. MacNeil. 1986. *The Story of English.* New York: Viking Penguin.

Moates, L. C. 1991. "Spelling Disability in Adolescents and Adults." In *Written Language Disorders: Theory into Practice,* edited by A. M. Bain, L. L. Bailet, and L. C. Moates, 23–42. Austin, Texas: Pro-Ed.

Stratton, J., and M. Montgomery. 1986. *The Fast-Track Program for Perfect Spelling.* New York: New American Library.

Troyka, L. Q. 1987. "Spelling and Hyphenation." In *A Handbook for Writers,* 385–408. Englewood Cliffs, N.J.: Prentice-Hall.

Authors

Patricia J. McAlexander is assistant professor in the English component of the University of Georgia's Division of Developmental Studies. A high school recipient of an award from NCTE, she received a B.A. in English and education from the State University of New York at Albany, an M.A. in English from Columbia University, and a Ph.D. in English from the University of Wisconsin. McAlexander has published articles on literature, composition, and learning disabilities in such journals as *Early American Literature, Studies in the Literary Imagination, College Composition and Communication*, and *Journal of Basic Writing*. Her interests in basic writing, learning disabilities, and spelling are reflected in this book.

Ann Brewster Dobie is professor of English at the University of Southwestern Louisiana, where she is director of Graduate Studies in Rhetoric and director of writing for Writing across the Curriculum. She is the author of numerous journal articles on composition and several writing textbooks, including *Comprehension and Composition*. Most recently, she has worked with Lynn Troyka in the preparation of the annotated instructor's edition of *Handbook for Writers*. In the spring of 1991, she brought out a collection of short fiction entitled *Something in Common: Contemporary Louisiana Stories*. A companion volume of poetry will be published in 1992.

Noel Gregg is the director of the University of Georgia Learning Disabilities Adult Clinic and associate professor in the Department of Special Education. She received her B.S. from James Madison University, her M.Ed. from the University of Virginia, and her Ph.D. from Northwestern University. Her Ph.D. was in communication disorders/learning disabilities, with minors in written language disorders and educational law. She has published articles concerning written language disorders in such journals as the *Journal of Basic Writing; Reading and Writing: An Interdisciplinary Journal;* the *Journal of Learning Disabilities: A Multidisciplinary Journal;* and the *British Columbia Journal of Special Education*. She has recently published chapters in two textbooks concerning the area of written expression disorders. Her special interest concerns assessment and interventions appropriate for adults with learning disabilities demonstrating specific written language disorders.